"I can't imagine a pastor who would not want to use this outstanding resource for establishing a mentoring ministry. The Parrotts have crafted a program that holds the potential for strengthening marriages through an entire congregation."

JOHN C. MAXWELL, AUTHOR OF *DEVELOPING THE LEADER WITHIN YOU*

"Les and Leslie know firsthand the ins and outs of setting up an effective mentoring ministry. They've made it easy to practice an idea that is long overdue ... the Parrotts' marriage mentoring curriculum is a must."

H. NORMAN WRIGHT, FOUNDER OF CHRISTIAN MARRIAGE ENRICHMENT

"Les and Leslie Parrott have produced an important guide for both pastors and mentoring couples. They are national pioneers of the new field of marriage mentoring."

MICHAEL J. MCMANUS, AUTHOR OF *MARRIAGE SAVERS*

"This book will serve as a tipping point in our collective efforts to turn back the tide of divorce. But more than that, countless marriages will be moved from good to great. The time is ripe for marriage mentoring and this book is exactly what we need."

GARY SMALLEY, AUTHOR OF *THE DNA OF RELATIONSHIPS*

"This book is long overdue and Les and Leslie Parrott are the perfect authors for it. Their passion for marriage mentoring has been evident for years and their expertise on the subject is unrivaled. I can't imagine a church that would not want to implement the mentoring ministry the Parrotts prescribe in this practical book. It's desperately needed. Whether you are a pastor or a layperson, already up and running with a marriage mentoring ministry, or just curious to know what it's all about — you can't afford to miss out on this fantastic resource."

GARY CHAPMAN, AUTHOR OF *THE FIVE LOVE LANGUAGES*

"Barb and I have had the wonderful privilege of serving as marriage mentors. But how we wish we could have had this incredible book to use as our guide! This must-have resource, packed with tips and resources, will empower and enable you as a marriage mentor — while giving you the added blessing of improving your own marriage."

WALT LARIMORE, MD, FAMILY PHYSICIAN, MEDICAL JOURNALIST, AND
BESTSELLING AUTHOR OF *GOD'S DESIGN FOR THE HIGHLY HEALTHY PERSON*

"Les and Leslie have a passion for marriage. There are few people I know more equipped to coach people into healthy, God-honoring intimacy. If churches would become marriage mentoring centers, it would create a revolution in our society."

JOHN ORTBERG, TEACHING PASTOR, MENLO PARK PRESBYTERIAN CHURCH

Resources by Les and Leslie Parrott

Books

Becoming Soul Mates
The Complete Guide to Marriage Mentoring
Getting Ready for the Wedding
I Love You More (and workbooks)
Just the Two of Us
Love Is
The Love List
Love Talk (and workbooks)
The Marriage Mentor Manual
Meditations on Proverbs for Couples
Pillow Talk
Questions Couples Ask
Relationships (and workbook)
Saving Your Marriage Before It Starts (and workbooks)
Saving Your Second Marriage Before It Starts (and workbooks)

Video Curriculum — ZondervanGroupware™

I Love You More
Love Talk
Mentoring Engaged and Newlywed Couples
Relationships
Saving Your Marriage Before It Starts

Audio Pages®

Love Talk
Relationships
Saving Your Marriage Before It Starts
Saving Your Second Marriage Before It Starts

Books by Les Parrott

The Control Freak
Helping Your Struggling Teenager
High Maintenance Relationships
The Life You Want Your Kids to Live
Seven Secrets of a Healthy Dating Relationship
Shoulda, Coulda, Woulda
Once Upon a Family
25 Ways to Win with People (coauthored with John Maxwell)
Love the Life You Live (coauthored with Neil Clark Warren)

Books by Leslie Parrott

If You Ever Needed Friends, It's Now
God Loves You Nose to Toes (children's book)
Marshmallow Clouds

Drs. Les & Leslie Parrott

CONNECTING
COUPLES TO
BUILD BETTER
MARRIAGES

THE
COMPLETE
GUIDE *to*
MARRIAGE
MENTORING

ZONDERVAN®

GRAND RAPIDS, MICHIGAN 49530 USA

ZONDERVAN.COM/
AUTHOR**TRACKER**

We want to hear from you. Please send your comments about this book to us in care of zreview@zondervan.com. Thank you.

ZONDERVAN®

The Complete Guide to Marriage Mentoring
Copyright © 2005 by The Foundation for Healthy Relationships

Requests for information should be addressed to:
Zondervan, *Grand Rapids, Michigan 49530*

Library of Congress Cataloging-in-Publication Data

Parrott, Les.
    The complete guide to marriage mentoring : connecting couples to build better marriages / Les and Leslie Parrott ; foreword by Gary Smalley.— 1st ed.
      p. cm.
    Includes bibliographical references and index.
    ISBN-13: 978-0-310-27046-1
    ISBN-10: 0-310-27046-4
    1. Church work with married people. 2. Mentoring in church work.
I. Parrott, Leslie L., 1964– II. Title.
BV4012.27.P36 2005
259'.14—dc22

                                                              2005020701

This edition printed on acid-free paper.

All Scripture quotations, unless otherwise indicated, are taken from the *Holy Bible: New International Version®*. NIV®. Copyright © 1973, 1978, 1984 by International Bible Society. Used by permission of Zondervan. All rights reserved.

Scripture quotations marked LB are taken from *The Living Bible*. Copyright © 1971 by Tyndale House Publishers, Inc., Wheaton, Illinois. All rights reserved.

Some anecdotes in this book are composites of real situations, but names, facts, and issues have been changed to protect confidentiality.

The website addresses recommended throughout this book are offered as a resource to you. These websites are not intended in any way to be or imply an endorsement on the part of Zondervan, nor do we vouch for their content for the life of this book.

All rights reserved. No part of this publication may be reproduced, stored in a retrieval system, or transmitted in any form or by any means—electronic, mechanical, photocopy, recording, or any other—except for brief quotations in printed reviews, without the prior permission of the publisher.

Published in association with Yates & Yates, LLP, Attorneys and Counselors, Suite 1000, Literary Agent, Orange, CA.

Interior design by Beth Shagene

Printed in the United States of America

---

09 10 11 • 23 22 21 20 19 18 17 16 15 14 13 12 11 10 9 8 7

To Jeff and Stacy Kemp
A couple whose passion
for building better marriages is an inspiration.

CONTENTS

PART THREE:

THE ESSENTIAL SKILLS FOR MARRIAGE MENTORING

APPENDIXES FOR MARRIAGE MENTORS

APPENDIXES FOR PASTORS
AND MARRIAGE MENTOR LEADERS

FOREWORD
BY GARY SMALLEY

Norma and I have known Les and Leslie Parrott for years. I laugh more with Les Parrott than just about anyone I know. We've traveled together for speaking engagements—a surefire way for getting to know each other well! We've done radio and television interviews together. We've shared writing ideas. We've enjoyed a myriad of meals in countless cities. And, though we live in different parts of the country, we've been in each other's homes. The point is that I know Les and Leslie, not only as professionals, but as people. Real people. I've seen them up close. I've witnessed their marriage. In short, I know their hearts.

In some respects, Norma and I have been long-distance marriage mentors to Les and Leslie. And I want you to know that this book on marriage mentoring comes straight from their core. To be honest, they could have easily written other books that would have had a wider appeal. But they wrote this book, quite literally, because God wanted them to. They are called to marriage mentoring. As Les has told me, "It's one of the reasons we are on this planet." I don't think it's an exaggeration to say they are fanatical about helping churches launch and sustain effective marriage mentoring ministries. That's why they have poured themselves into this immensely helpful book. And I, for one, could not be more grateful.

I believe that this book, along with other mentoring resources by the Parrotts, will serve as a tipping point in our collective efforts to turn back the tide of divorce. But more than that, I believe that through what they call "the boomerang effect," countless marriages will also be moved from good to great. The time is ripe for marriage mentoring and this book is exactly what we need.

In many ways, this is a book that only the Parrotts could write. Why? Because it's an idea they birthed more than a dozen years ago. They are marriage mentoring pioneers. While the concept of marriage mentoring may be relatively new to you, it's one that Les and Leslie have been steeped in.

The Parrotts have been talking about marriage mentoring for more than a decade—long before most of us had even heard of it. They have trained numerous couples across North America, mentored dozens of couples themselves, and have been mentored at nearly every turn in their own marriage. They know the value of this effort from every angle.

And so it is with great pleasure that I join the Parrotts in helping them to realize their God-given dream of seeing a million marriage mentors rise up in the local church. I believe it will happen. I believe marriage mentoring is the lost key, now recovered, that the church has been desperate to find. And it will be because of couples like you—marriage mentors—that more and more marriages will become what God intended. So, join the Parrotts and me, and a host of others, to form a powerful safety net supporting couples in your community and beyond. This effort just may become the single greatest social revolution in history, impacting couples and families for generations.

As you read through the chapters of this practical book you'll soon see that the Parrotts have made marriage mentoring easy. They've given us the tools. All we have to do is use them.

I pray you will.

Gary Smalley
Branson, Missouri

ACKNOWLEDGMENTS

More people than we can name have helped us to make this book far better than we could have made it on our own. We have received input and feedback from literally hundreds of people across North America on this project and it's impossible to identify everyone. However, we feel compelled to express deep appreciation to those who readily come to mind.

As always, we begin with a huge thank-you to our Zondervan team that includes Bruce Ryskamp, Doug Lockhart, Scott Bolinder, Lyn Cryderman, Stan Gundry, Sandy Vander Zicht, Greg Clouse, John Topliff, Greg Steilstra, Joyce Ondersma, Jackie Aldridge, Mark Hunt, John Raymond, T. J. Rathbun, Amy Boucher Pye, and Vicki Cessna. In addition, we were fortunate to have Paul Engle come aboard for this project and we could not be more grateful for his encouraging spirit and valuable expertise. Everyone at Zondervan quickly caught the vision for this book. Right from the start, it was apparent that this was a special effort that we all believed would not only change how many churches minister to couples but that it would eventually change many, many marriages. It is a book that was conceived at a conference table in Grand Rapids and it has been surrounded by a multitude of prayers ever since.

Our RealRelationships team is stellar. Janice Lundquist, Jayme Stevens, Robin Schults, Mike Burak, Doug McKinley, and Kevin Small are simply the best. Each contributes their best gifts and graces to our efforts, making what we do immeasurably easier and more effective. We can't say thanks enough.

We owe a special thanks to Shane Fookes. What a blessing he has been and continues to be in helping us make our mentoring tools sound, functional, and accessible. His heartfelt passion is a gift to our efforts and often fuels our own passion for this ministry—especially after the long, late-night hours of crafting the words in these chapters. He has read them all and made our message stronger. Much stronger. We are deeply grateful to Shane.

Though we are certain to leave individuals out of this list we want to also note everyone we can who has offered input from the front lines of marriage mentoring: Jason Krafsky, Jeff Kemp, John Erwin, Steve Wages, Kristin Byington, Tim Popadic, Jim Supp, Jim Mueller, Patti Anderson, Gary Collins, Michael Sytsma, Jennifer Ripley, Ev Worthington, John Swope, Scott Stanley, Steve Wright, Kriss Bottino, Dennis Rainey, Irv Woolf, Greg Hasek, Mike Sciarra, Judi Hoefs, Gary Smalley, Gil Stuart, Brenda Stuart, Gail Hatmaker, Doug Engberg, Megan Millar, Steve Moore, Ken Coleman, Jeff McFarlane, Kathy Lunn, Debbie Daniels, Rodney Cox, Paul Casey, Bonnie Brann, Jack Hardcastle, Carri Taylor, Joneal Kirby, Kent Dyer, Grant Fishbook, Rob Berreth, David Olson. Whether it was formal or informal, each of you has offered specific advice and critique of various components of this book and we want you to know how valuable your contribution is to us.

Finally, we want to thank the hundreds, if not thousands, of marriage mentors we have trained, interviewed, and learned from over the years — as well as the pastors who have caught the vision for what marriage mentoring can do in the local church. You are the reason we wrote this book.

Les and Leslie Parrott
Seattle, Washington

A PERSONAL WORD
TO MARRIAGE MENTORS

The film *Pearl Harbor* tells the story of two friends, Rafe, played by Ben Affleck, and Danny, played by Josh Hartnett, who survive the attack on Pearl Harbor and enter into World War II as fighter pilots.

In response to the Japanese attack, the Americans plan a risky, top-secret strike on Japan. Knowing the danger, Rafe and Danny are recruited for this mission, called the Doolittle Raid. Because of the tremendous risk, Colonel Jimmy Doolittle gives every pilot the choice to back out, but they all volunteer.

On the aircraft carrier en route to Japan, Rafe and Danny are painting logos on their airplanes when Danny quips: "Hey, Red, you think they picked us because we're young and dumb?"

"No, Goose. We're the tip of the sword," says Rafe.

Colonel Doolittle, off in the shadows, looks at his two key pilots and tells his fellow commander, "We may lose this battle, but we're going to win this war. You know how I know?"

"No, how?"

Doolittle points at Rafe and Danny. "Them. Because they are rare. At times like these you see them stepping forward." After a long pause, he adds, "There's nothing stronger than the heart of a volunteer."

And he's right. You wouldn't be reading these words if you didn't understand this powerful sentiment. You have the heart of a volunteer. As a couple who is interested in marriage mentoring, you know that you can make a difference. You know that you can help win the war on divorce and empower couples to build rock-solid relationships.

And while the difference you make may be one couple at a time, we are here to tell you that you are the tip of the sword. As marriage mentors, you are on the front lines of one of the most important battles the church has ever faced, namely a skyrocketing divorce rate. Divorce is a stealthy enemy permeating the walls of today's church. In fact, the divorce rate is just as high for committed Christians as it is for anyone else.

But not for long!

That's precisely why you have been recruited. Maybe your pastor asked you to take a look at this book and consider how you might be involved in a marriage mentoring ministry. Or maybe you volunteered yourself and are already deeply involved as a marriage mentor couple, recruiting and training others in the effort. Or perhaps you're somewhere in between. Whatever your situation, this book is designed to thoroughly equip you for this critically important mission. If the war against failing marriages is to be won, if we are to reduce the divorce rate inside and outside the church, it will be because of volunteers like you who are the tip of the sword.

You are desperately needed. And as you will see in this book you don't have to have all the answers or be the perfect couple to make a difference. Far from it. In fact, Martin Luther, the great church reformer, recognized in Scripture a call of the "priesthood of all believers." God calls every person, wherever they are in the body of Christ, to some kind of ministry. We are thrilled to know that you're considering the call of marriage mentoring.

A PERSONAL WORD
TO PASTORS

When President Ronald Reagan was a teenager in Dixon, Illinois, he had a summer job as a lifeguard on the treacherous Rock River. One day from his elevated perch at Lowell Park, he noticed one of Dixon's most popular girls waving at him from the water.

"At least I thought she was waving," Reagan recalls. "My chest puffed out a little, and I waved back. Then I turned away for a moment. When I looked again, she was going down. She had tried to signal for help."

Ever felt like the young Ronald Reagan in that moment? Whether you know it or not, some people in your congregation may not look particularly needy or desperate for help, but many of them are. Countless couples, on any given weekend, file into churches across the country, looking their "Sunday best," and quietly keeping a marriage problem to themselves. The stigma of counseling may be keeping them from seeking help. Or they may feel all alone, that nobody else would understand. Or they may simply have nobody to talk to. But truth be told, some of these couples are going down. Their marriages are hurting and nobody has recognized their signal for help—and even if they have, they don't feel it's their place to step in.

Surely you've witnessed a painful divorce where trouble was never suspected. You've certainly seen the newlywed couple, full of promise, whose marriage is short-lived because they didn't get a solid start. And think of the numerous couples in your care who are stuck in a rut, not reaching their full potential.

Now, think of the difference it would make if these couples in your congregation could be linked with other couples, more seasoned and experienced in what these couples are going through. Would it make any difference? You bet. How do we know? Because we've been recruiting, screening, and training couples to become marriage mentors for more than a decade. We've heard their stories. We've done the research. Marriage mentoring works.

Of course, you may already be aware of the power of marriage mentoring. Or maybe you're just now learning about it. Either way, *The Complete Guide to Marriage Mentoring* will provide you with everything you need to begin a ministry or to maximize it.

Both of us grew up in a parsonage. We've been involved in church work our entire lives. Les is an ordained minister. We also speak to hundreds of ministers annually. So we know you may have some reticence. You may be saying, "I don't need another program to administer." You're right. That's why marriage mentoring is low-maintenance. It belongs to the laity. Or maybe you're saying "I can't get volunteers to teach classes, let alone mentor other couples." We understand. But we'll show you how recruiting mentor couples is easier than you think. Perhaps you're saying, "I don't want to detract from the marriage counseling program we've built up." It won't. In fact, it will augment it. "For now we're putting our energies into children's ministry and youth work." Worthy indeed. But marriage mentoring may be the most important thing you ever do for the young people in your church. Marriage mentoring can literally increase the spiritual vitality of your entire congregation.

The truth is, we can't think of a legitimate excuse for not having a marriage mentoring ministry in *every* local church, large or small. Why? Because couples of every age and stage can benefit from marriage mentoring and it's easy for the local church to get going.

Not only that, but the Bible calls us to this kind of action. Marriage mentoring is a means by which you can fulfill Paul's injunction when he says the job of a pastor is "to prepare God's people for works of service" (Ephesians 4:12). What works of service could be of more value these days to the couples in your care than marriage mentoring?

We are honored and humbled that you are taking the time to peruse this book—and perhaps provide copies to your mentors and potential mentors. In it we've aimed our writing directly to marriage mentors, but we have a special section at the end specifically for you and for the leaders of your marriage mentoring program. It includes some hands-on resources that will equip you for this vital ministry. For we know it will be through ministers like you that God will empower the church to cut the divorce rate, heal wounded couples, and revolutionize relationships.

We wish you every success in your efforts for doing just that.

THE SLEEPING GIANT
IN THE CHURCH

I believe a very large majority of churchgoers are merely slumbering.
CHARLES HADDON SPURGEON

In his book *Did You Spot the Gorilla?* psychologist Richard Wiseman describes an experiment where volunteers watched a thirty-second video of two teams playing basketball and were asked to count the number of times one of the teams passed the ball. What they weren't told was that halfway through the video, a man dressed in a gorilla suit would run onto the court, stand in front of the camera, and beat his chest. Amazingly only a few of the volunteers spotted the man in the gorilla suit. Most of the volunteers were so intent on counting passes that they completely missed the gorilla.

Wiseman concluded that most people go through life so focused on the task at hand they completely miss what would otherwise be obvious. Has the church fallen victim to this same phenomenon? Are we blind to the gorilla of marriage mentoring? After all, it's a slumbering giant visible in every congregation—a team of couples who have what it takes to make a powerful

> *I am only one, but I am one.*
> *I can't do everything,*
> *but I can do something. And*
> *what I can do, I ought to do.*
> *And what I ought to do, by*
> *the Grace of God, I shall do.*
> EDWARD EVERETT HALE

impact on marriages around them. And yet, for the most part, they haven't been tapped. They've been neglected or unrecognized.

This book is designed to change all that. It's designed to awaken the sleeping giant of marriage mentors in the local church and enable them to seize an opportunity that has been too long neglected.

Consider the facts. There are close to 400,000 churches in America.[1] If just one-third of these churches would recruit and train ten mentor couples each, that would mean one million marriage mentors. Think of the difference that would make! With a mighty band of marriage mentors we could surely save half of the 1.2 million marriages that end in divorce each year. And think of the marriages that could move from good to great if only they had another couple with more experience to walk beside them.

Truth be told, they do. Every congregation, no matter how big or small, has the potential to awaken the marriage mentors in its midst. With far too many marriages suffering in silence and with far too many couples merely getting by, it's high time we, the church, do something. And we can.

WE MUST DO SOMETHING

One morning, near the turn of the twentieth century, Bramwell Booth visited his elderly father, William Booth, founder of the Salvation Army.

"Bramwell, did you know that men slept out all night on the bridges?" William had arrived in London very late the night before from a town in the south of England and had to cross through the capital to reach his home. What he had seen on that midnight return accounted for his inquiry.

"Well, yes," Bramwell replied, "a lot of poor fellows, I suppose, do that."

"Then go and do something!" William said. "We must do something."

"What can we do?"

"Get them shelter."

"That will cost money."

"Something must be done. Get hold of a warehouse and warm it, and find something to cover them!"

That was the beginning of the Salvation Army shelters. And if William Booth was alive today he just might have the same passion for "doing something" about the sad state of marriage. And make no mistake about it, the state of marriage is sad.

We've all heard the startling statistics of divorce. Almost anyone can tell you that "half of all marriages end in divorce." We're almost immune to the numbers. It gets a little closer to home when you ask an average congregation to raise their hands if they have had someone in their family or a close friend suffer a divorce. Nearly every hand goes up. We all know something needs to be done, but for the most part we haven't known what to do. Or worse, we think very little or nothing can be done.

> *I took the road less traveled by, and that has made all the difference.*
> ROBERT FROST

But by now, you know that we beg to differ with this stance. Something can be done. And something is already being done in many churches around North America. Let us tell you what we mean.

OUR STORY

Fifteen years ago we first began using the term *marriage mentors* in relationship to a program we developed called *Saving Your Marriage Before It Starts*. Through a seminar we launched in Seattle we were beginning to help hundreds of newlyweds get started on the right foot. But soon into our efforts we began to wonder whether the information we were teaching was actually sticking. We began to wonder how we could build in some accountability for these couples who went through our program, to be sure they were actually putting the information into practice. There were too many for us to follow up on personally, so we began to recruit older, more experienced couples, to meet with these newlyweds. Without much training at first, we asked them to simply check in with their assigned couple every so often to see how things were going. And it didn't take us long to realize that something exciting was happening because of this fledgling notion. We were beginning to hear remarkable stories convincing us that the time-honored tool of mentoring is more than ready to be applied to marriage.

Tom and Wendy, a typical newly married couple, were among the first to experience our program. In their mid-twenties, they had dated for nearly two years before getting engaged. They had the blessing of their parents, attended premarital counseling, and were on their way to living happily ever after — or so everyone thought.

But marriage for Tom and Wendy, like the majority of newlyweds, wasn't all they hoped for. Each of them, for different reasons, felt a bit slighted. Unlike the majority of couples, however, Tom and Wendy talked openly about their feelings. The expectations they had of marriage were not getting met and they were determined to do something about it. So on a cold January day, eight months after their wedding, Tom and Wendy asked for help.

THE GUINEA PIG COUPLE

Bundled up against the cold, they came into our office and began to shed their coats. As Wendy sipped hot coffee to thaw out, she said: "We have talked to friends and family about what is going on, but we both decided we needed more objectivity."

Tom joined in: "Yeah, everybody who knows us just says 'give it time' or something like that." Their marriage, he went on to say, was not suffering a major trauma; it didn't need an overhaul, just "a little realignment."

We met with Tom and Wendy for nearly an hour, listening to their experience. We gave them a couple of exercises to help them explore their misconceptions of marriage and we recommended a few resources. Then we talked about the idea of linking up with a marriage mentor couple.

"What's that?" they both asked.

We told them how meeting from time to time with a more seasoned married couple could give them a sounding board and a safe place to explore some of their questions about marriage. Like most newlyweds we talk to, Tom and Wendy were very eager to find such a couple. After a bit of discussion, they suggested a married couple in their church. Neither of them knew the couple very well, but they respected their marriage from afar and thought they would fit the bill. After a couple of phone calls and a little more exploration, we made the connection for Tom and Wendy. Over the course of several months, they met several times with their mentors, Nate and Sharon.

> *People are not very good at taking orders but they are great at imitating.*
> WAYMAN MITCHELL

Tom and Wendy found the marriage mentoring extremely helpful. Here is a portion of a letter they wrote to us back then:

> *Dear Les and Leslie,*
>
> How can we ever thank you for helping us find a marriage mentor couple. Before coming to you we had never even heard of such an idea. But needless to say, our mentoring relationship with Nate and Sharon ended up being the most important thing we have ever done to build up our marriage. It was so nice to have another couple know what we were going through and remain objective at the same time.
>
> We have since moved to another state, but on our wedding anniversary, Nate and Sharon always give us a call to celebrate our marriage.
>
> Anyway, we are writing to say thank you and to say that you should tell more people about the benefits of marriage mentoring. Someday we hope to give back the gift that Nate and Sharon gave to us by mentoring some newly married couples. We think every couple just starting out should have a mentor.

That's not a bad idea, we thought to ourselves. And we've made it standard practice ever since for every newlywed couple who has been part of our *Saving Your Marriage Before It Starts* program. We have literally linked thousands of newlyweds with mentors over the last decade.

HOW THEY'RE DOING TODAY

As we were writing this chapter we began to get curious about Tom and Wendy, so we tracked them down. Now living in Portland, Oregon, Wendy and Tom have been married fifteen years and have two children. They are not the perfect couple, but they are madly in love and happier than they ever imagined. In an email we received from Wendy just this week she revealed a "secret" to their success.

> As one of the first couples in your group to go though the mentoring process we became quick converts. We immediately saw the advantage to having Nate and Sharon, a couple we didn't even know at the start, in our lives. They made a world of difference for us.
>
> And you might be pleased to know that we've followed up on our intentions to give back what they gave to us. A few years ago we began to do some mentoring ourselves. Our church didn't have a mentoring program and we thought it was time that they did—so we started one. We now have six other mentoring couples who work with us and we're having a blast. As Tom often says, "It's the best thing we do all year for our own marriage." He's right. Meeting with our mentorees brings us closer together and it feels so right to know we are doing some good . . . just like Nate and Sharon did for us.
>
> By the way, they still send us an anniversary card every year!

As you might imagine, this email was certainly encouraging and timely. Because of Tom and Wendy, and thousands of couples we've met with just like them, we come to the enterprise of marriage mentoring with great conviction and passion. And with a vision for what might be.

OUR DREAM

We have a dream that one day a massive network of marriage mentors will undergird the state of marriage across North America and around the world. Serving as a type of relational safety net, these mentors will lift up and support couples at crucial crossroads—those just starting out, about to have a baby, in crisis, raising teenagers, looking to maximize their marriage, whatever. Marriage mentoring applies to every stage and phase of married life.

It's a dream we've been talking about wherever we can. In fact, just a few years ago, the governor of Oklahoma invited us to move to his state (where they have one of the highest divorce rates in the country) for one year. And we did. Why? It gave us the opportunity to meet with hundreds of clergy and thousands of lay couples just to talk about our dream of marriage mentoring. We've also talked about it on national radio and television. We've spoken about it in dozens of conferences. We've written about it in numerous magazines and newspapers.

We've been preaching "marriage mentoring" for so long in so many places with so little repercussion that we sometimes wondered if anyone was listening. But no longer.

We are encouraged. Very encouraged. More than ever, we are seeing the church awaken to this idea and catch on to this dream. In fact, we now receive emails every day with requests for more information on marriage mentoring. If you Google "marriage mentoring" your search will return over a half million webpages dealing with the idea in some fashion. More and more churches identify themselves as having a marriage mentoring ministry. And in a recent survey, 62 percent of respondents said they'd like to find a mentor couple in their church and 92 percent said they would especially like to have a mentor to help them through times of conflict.[2]

The times are changing. In 1995 we published a little book called *The Marriage Mentor Manual* and produced a videotape series to accompany it. Since then, little else has been written or produced for marriage mentors. That's why we felt compelled to write this book and develop a forthcoming contemporary DVD series as well as set up a website at www.RealRelationships.com. This book and the resources in the appendixes can be used independently. But they are also an important part of a related set of tools designed to equip church leaders and marriage mentors to either set up a marriage mentoring program for the first time or improve the marriage mentoring already established in your church.

We're hearing the rumblings of a sleeping giant about to wake up. And we're going to do everything we can to meet its needs.

PART ONE

The BIG PICTURE *on* MARRIAGE MENTORING

Wisdom, like an inheritance, is a good thing.
ECCLESIASTES 7:11

Can you imagine giving an inheritance to another couple—a couple not related to you? It's an unusual gift, indeed, but that's exactly what you'll be doing as a marriage mentor. As you pour your wisdom into another couple who has not yet traveled the distance you have in your own marriage, you'll impart an invaluable gift that this couple would never receive on their own. That's why we're thrilled at the thought of your interest in marriage mentoring. We also believe you'll find it to be one of the most rewarding activities your marriage will ever enjoy.

Before we reveal the fringe benefits to your own relationship however (see chapter 4), we want to be sure you begin this journey with the big picture in view. So, we'll explain exactly what we mean by marriage mentoring, show you what the role entails, and clue you in to how you can avoid the common mistakes some beginning marriage mentors make.

CHAPTER 1

WHAT MARRIAGE MENTORING IS AND ISN'T

Mentoring is a brain to pick, a shoulder to cry on, and a kick in the pants.
JOHN C. CROSBY

Even though Rodger and Lynne Schmidt had their sights set on going to Africa as missionaries, they still struggled. "Is this really something we should be doing?" they were asking themselves.

Erik Johnson tells their story in an article he wrote for *Leadership Journal*.[1] "At the same time in the same city, another couple was also wrestling with their call, though from the other end of a missionary career. Now retired, this couple was asking, 'After forty-one years as missionaries in Africa, who are we? Our home and life work are on another continent. What is our life all about?'"

A mentoring program at Denver Seminary brought these two couples together. And it was a great match. Through this mentoring relationship, the Schmidts' call was confirmed, and the retired couple discovered a profound sense of significance in their new role as mentors. "We felt encouraged, they felt validated," notes Rodger Schmidt.

And so go the benefits of mentoring.

In this chapter we begin by touching on the immense need for mentors in today's culture. From there we ask what is a mentor in general and then we get specific by exploring exactly what marriage mentoring is and isn't. Finally, we attempt to define the mentoring relationship itself.

TODAY'S NEED FOR MENTORS

Why do the trades have apprenticeships and professions require internships? Because personal attention from experienced practitioners helps learners master essential skills, techniques, attitudes, and knowledge.

In every culture throughout human history, mentoring has been the primary means of passing on knowledge and skills. In the past, mentoring took place in the university where a student learned directly from the scholar. It took place in the studio where the artist poured himself into the formation of his protégés.

> *Mentoring involves life-to-life exchanges that help others discover and pursue their passions and sort out their priorities.*
>
> DAVID STODDARD

The Bible is certainly filled with examples of mentoring: Eli and Samuel, Elijah and Elisha, Moses and Joshua, Naomi and Ruth, Elizabeth and Mary, Barnabas and Paul, Paul and Timothy. And, of course, Jesus and the disciples is a supreme example of mentoring.

Down through the centuries, young people have learned most through careful observation of those more experienced. Up until recently, mentoring was a way of life between the generations. But today, mentoring, for the most part, is in short supply. Mentoring was once assumed, expected, and therefore, almost unnoticed because of its commonness. But in the modern age, the learning process has shifted. It now relies primarily on computers, classrooms, books, and media. In most cases today, the relational connection between the knowledge-and-experience giver and the receiver has weakened or is nonexistent.

The time has come to bring back the fine art of mentoring.

WHAT IS A MENTOR?

Does mentoring's near disappearance mean it is no longer helpful? Absolutely not. Ask any successful leader and he or she will tell you: a young person starting out in a career, for example, will benefit greatly from a mentor—an older, experienced person who knows the ropes and will teach a protégé how things are done.

Here's a pop quiz question:

A mentor is . . .
   a) A model
   b) An encourager
   c) An imparter of knowledge
   d) All of the above

The answer is "d." A mentor may wear many different hats but the one thing that all mentors share is the ability to listen and encourage. A mentor is "a brain to pick, an ear to listen, and a push in the right direction," according to the Uncommon Individual Foundation, an organization devoted to mentoring research and training. It reports that mentoring is one of the most powerful tools we have for influencing human behavior.

The term *mentor* arises from an unlikely source. It first appeared in Homer's classic, *The Odyssey*, where Odysseus asked a wise man named Mentor to care for his son, Telemachus, while Odysseus was off fighting in the Trojan War. Mentor taught the boy "not only in book learning but also in the wiles of the world." The fabled Mentor must have done his job well, because Telemachus grew up to be an enterprising lad who gallantly helped his father recover his kingdom.

But mentoring is more than the stuff of legends. A real-life mentor, one who serves as a model and provides individualized help and encouragement, can be invaluable to a receptive mentoree. Among the most important roles mentors play include:

- giving timely information to mentorees
- modeling aspects of what they wish to impart
- challenging and motivating mentorees to move to higher levels
- directing mentorees to helpful resources when needed (sometimes painfully so)
- encouraging goodness and inspiring greatness
- lessening mentorees' anxiety by normalizing experiences
- helping mentorees set goals
- keeping mentorees accountable to their goals
- providing a periodic review and evaluation of mentorees' performance

A word of caution is in order: Mentors can do all of the aforementioned things and still be ineffective. Two dynamics are vital to the success of any mentoring relationship. Without them, all the modeling, challenging, encouraging, goal-setting, and accountability will fall flat. The two critical dynamics are (1) attraction, and (2) responsiveness.

Attraction is the starting point in every effective mentoring relationship. The mentor and the mentoree must be drawn to each other to some degree. If either side is not genuinely interested in the other, true mentoring will never take place. Along with this attractiveness, the mentoree must be willing and ready to learn from the mentor. Without a responsive attitude and a receptive spirit on the part of the mentoree, little genuine mentoring can occur.

WHAT IS A MARRIAGE MENTOR?

Through our Center for Relationship Development we have helped coordinate thousands of marriage mentoring relationships over the years and we know firsthand how beneficial this relationship can be. We've heard countless stories. We've followed hundreds of these relationships. And we've come to a conclusion: there is no single way to be a marriage mentor; every mentoring relationship takes on its own personality. Yet the variance in these relationships still operates within certain parameters and that's what allows us to define our terms.

So here goes. We define a marriage mentor as *a relatively happy, more experienced couple purposefully investing in another couple to effectively navigate a journey that they have already taken.*

Mentor: Someone whose hindsight can become your foresight.

ANONYMOUS

It is a broad definition because, as we just mentioned, there is no one right way to mentor. Each mentoring relationship takes on its own style. The amount of time couples spend together and the content they discuss is personalized to that relationship. A marriage mentoring relationship can be short term or long term. It can be consistent and predictable or spontaneous and sporadic.

While every marriage mentoring relationship has its own style that unfolds as the relationship develops, some potential confusion can be spared if the mentors and mentorees discuss their initial expectations of the relationship. This discussion, of course, necessitates the mentoring couple to be somewhat clear on their own "style" before meeting with the mentorees. For example, you may want to discuss whether you see yourselves more as models or as coaches or as teachers or as guides, and so on.

For now, here is a representative list of what a marriage mentor couple does. A marriage mentor couple:

- willingly shares what they know (in a noncompetitive way)
- represents skill, knowledge, virtue, and accomplishment because they have gone before the couple they are mentoring
- takes a personal and heartfelt interest in the other couple's development and well-being
- offers support, challenge, patience, and enthusiasm while guiding other couples to new levels of competence
- points the way and represents tangible evidence of what another couple can become

- exposes the recipients of their mentoring to new ideas, perspectives, and standards
- has more expertise in terms of knowledge yet views themselves as equal to those they mentor

The point is that each marriage mentor couple needs to consider what it is that they want to bring to the mentoring relationship. This means considering your two personalities and traits. Importantly, it also means being clear about what your role as a mentor couple does *not* include.

WHAT A MENTOR IS NOT

"What I need is someone to talk to who has walked down the path I'm just beginning," said Lisa, four months into her new marriage. "Whenever I go to my mom or dad with a situation, they end up parenting me or teaching me something I don't really need to learn."

Lisa, like most newlyweds we have met, needs a mentor. Mom and Dad certainly serve a helpful function in the life of a new bride or groom, but they cannot usually offer the distance and objectivity that a mentor gives. For this reason, it is important to realize exactly what a mentor is not.

The following is a list of mistaken mentoring roles we have witnessed, offered as a guide to keeping you from making the same mistakes. A mentor is not:

> *Many of the best-intentioned efforts to foster new learning disciplines flounder because those leading the charge forget the first rule of learning: people learn what they need to learn, not what someone else thinks they need to learn.*
>
> PETER SENGE

- a mother or father. Your job is not to parent the couple you are mentoring.
- automatically a pal or a buddy. Your job is not necessarily to be friends for the purpose of socializing.
- "on call" for every little crisis. Your time is limited to discussion about major situations, not minor ones.
- necessarily committed long-term. The mentoring relationship may have a prescribed timeline or it may follow a natural cycle of its own.
- a professor. Your job it not to instruct in the traditional sense; you'll typically not need to prepare for your meetings or do any research. Your life experience is your teaching tool.

- a know-it-all. We'll have more to say about this later, but let's make it clear right now: your job is not to have all the answers.

We'll say it again. A marriage mentor is *a relatively happy, more experienced couple purposefully investing in another couple to effectively navigate a journey that they have already taken.*

THE MARRIAGE MENTOR'S MISSION

The Christian church has been built through a sense of mission.[2] The apostle Paul's mission was to proclaim the gospel to the Gentiles. John's mission was to teach the love of Christ. And when you consider Jesus' disciples you can clearly see they had a sense of mission. His first twelve followers were called to be fishers of people. When his seventy volunteers spread out across Galilee, their mission was to proclaim the kingdom of God. When Jesus prepared to leave his followers on the Mount of Olives, he gave them the Great Commission (Mark 16:15).

> *The passengers on the bus don't go to the Greyhound depot, walk up to the ticket window, and ask, "Which bus has the friendliest driver?" Instead, they ask for the bus that will get them to the desired destination. Before they buy a ticket and get on board, they want to know the direction the bus is going.*
>
> RICH DOEBLER

The first generation of Christians knew what their mission was. They were to go into all their world, preaching and teaching the gospel, baptizing believers, and gathering them into a church. This mission was translated into operational terms they could follow. Anywhere a Christian family moved, they started a meeting of believers in their own home. And for three hundred years, the "house church" was the only kind of church the Christian movement knew.

We believe strongly that the first priority for marriage mentors should be a well-defined mission. This mission needs to be clearly stated, enthusiastically accepted, and internally believed. To be effective, every couple who volunteers to mentor anther couple needs a strong sense of mission.

So what is that mission and purpose? We've talked to enough marriage mentoring churches to know that many have their own way of articulating this. But a vast majority of local marriage mentoring ministries have yet to define it.

As with any mission, the place to begin is with a simple sentence stem: "The purpose of marriage mentoring is...." Once you can complete this sentence clearly and with enthusiasm, you have locked onto your mission. To help you do just that, allow us to give you a starting place. After reviewing many local marriage mentoring ministries and talking with volunteers and pastors, we believe the following sentence captures the spirit and belief of what most are trying to accomplish.

> *The purpose of marriage mentoring is to lovingly invest*
> *in the preparation, maximization, and restoration of lifelong marriages*
> *by walking alongside couples who are less experienced than their mentors.*

Of course, you may find this purpose statement to be right in your sweet spot. Maybe it exactly captures what you are about. But feel free to edit it. Adapt it. Make it your own. The point is that for you as a couple to be great in your role as marriage mentors, you have to have a deep sense of your mission.

What Is a Marriage Mentor Relationship?

Before leaving this chapter, we also want to put a finer point on the marriage mentoring *relationship*. For make no mistake about it, this *is* a relationship and the mentorees shape it just as much as the mentors.

For our purposes, a marriage mentoring relationship *is intentionally established by mutual agreement between a more experienced couple and a less experienced couple for the purpose of helping the less experienced couple.*

Note that this relationship is *intentional*. It's premeditated, planned, and on purpose. It's also *mutually agreed upon*. Both couples know the purpose of the relationship. A true mentoring relationship does not happen incognito. You can't genuinely mentor a couple without them agreeing to it. And vice versa. You have to *want* to mentor the couple you're mentoring.

Also note that this definition highlights *experience*. Crucial to the success of the relationship is that the more experienced couple has traveled a road similar to the one the less experienced couple is traveling. They have knowledge and wisdom to impart because of

> *A mission statement has to be operational or otherwise it is just good intentions.*
>
> Peter Drucker

their experience. And while you, as the mentors, will certainly benefit from this relationship (we'll get to that in our chapter on the boomerang effect), *the relationship exists for the benefit of the less experienced couple.* As fellow marriage mentoring advocate Shane Fookes says, "It is the hunger of the younger that provides the energy, pace, and direction of the relationship."

All this defining brings us to an important question that you may be asking: Can anyone be a marriage mentor? We address this in the next chapter.

CHAPTER 2

CAN ANYONE BE A MARRIAGE MENTOR?

Be what you would have your pupils to be.
THOMAS CARLYLE

Meet Brian and Sarah, potential marriage mentors. Married for more than a decade, they have their ups and downs, but for the most part are happy together. From all appearances, they seem to have what it takes to be effective marriage mentors—with the exception of one thing. Brian, though bright and articulate, has a habit of making snap judgments. As Sarah sometimes puts it, Brian is trigger-happy with advice. While this trait is certainly helpful at times, he can come across as task-oriented and impatient. Can Brian and Sarah still be effective marriage mentors?

Meet Lisa and Ryan. Married fourteen years (this is Ryan's second marriage), they've done a terrific job of blending a family and have a passion for helping other couples do the same. They seem to be good marriage mentor candidates, but Lisa's greatest strength—her sensitivity to others' needs—is also a weakness that might potentially harm the couples they want to help: she cannot stand conflict of any kind and avoids it at all costs. She glosses over trouble spots, discounts disagreements, and sees everything as "great" even when a problem is obvious. Can Lisa and Ryan be effective marriage mentors?

So what do you think about Brian and Sarah? If you were in charge of screening marriage mentors in your local church, would they make the cut? How about Lisa and Ryan? Before you answer, let us introduce you to another couple volunteering to be marriage mentors.

Meet Ken and Tiffany. They've been married twenty-two years and have two daughters in college. As they enter the empty nest stage, they have a new interest in helping other couples who have struggled with the same serious hurdle—namely, infidelity. Both Ken and Tiffany have been unfaithful in their marriage over the years and they believe they know what can be done to help other couples who have experienced this heartache of betrayal. Tiffany's infidelity occurred more than fifteen years ago. So did Ken's. But he also had a one-night stand about nine months ago. Tiffany was understandably furious and had him move out of their house for several weeks. She's since forgiven him but the wound is still fresh. Are they in a place to mentor other couples on this issue?

The answer to this one is pretty clear, right? They need more time to resolve their own issues. Which brings us back to our first two couples. The answer for them, in our opinion, is a little more fuzzy. Can Brian learn to curtail his trigger-happy advice? Can Lisa learn to become more honest and comfortable with conflict? Maybe.

Anyone with a modicum of human warmth, common sense, some sensitivity to human problems, and a desire to help can benefit many.
JEROME D. FRANK

But let's back up to consider what character qualities are crucial for every marriage mentor. Then we'll explore the caution flags that may indicate a couple, at least for the time being, simply shouldn't make the cut. And we should emphasize here that the single most important factor in successful marriage mentoring is *who you are as a couple*. Regardless of your education, training, or relational skills, if you bring certain qualities into the mentoring relationship that are likely to detract from your purpose, the chances of creating an effective mentoring relationship diminish. There's no way around it.

THE EFFECTIVE MENTOR

Many researchers have attempted to identify the qualities that make up the successful mentor: sensitivity, hope, perspective, compassion, awareness, knowledge, patience, optimism, realism, perseverance, objectivity ... the list could fill several pages. However, when all of the traits are taken into account, three emerge as essential: warmth, genuineness, and empathy.

Warmth

Everyone knows what it feels like to be with someone who is warm. A mentor who possesses warmth brings a sense of relaxation and comfort to the relationship. They have an attitude that does not evaluate or require change. In short, they accept their mentorees right where they are. It's not that a mentor approves of everything a mentoree does; rather the marriage mentors simply accept the other couple — in spite of aspects of their behavior they may not necessarily like.

Imagine that you are mentoring a young couple, newly married, and soon into the mentoring relationship you discover that the husband brought into his new marriage several thousand dollars worth of debt. And his bride didn't know about this until the very moment you found out about it yourselves. Are you beginning to bristle? Of course! That's a sneaky and dishonorable maneuver. You can't blame the bride for being angry. Really angry! But what about you? Can you maintain your composure and objectivity? Can you keep your sense of personal warmth intact even in the midst of this startling news?

Of course, conveying warmth does not mean smothering your couple in sentimentality. Warmth simply conveys respect for them as human beings despite what they put on the table. It allows you to treat this new husband as a person of worth even though he did something shameful. Warmth allows a mentor to free a mentoree from trying to win approval. Without a generous supply of warmth, some mentoree couples will perform in order to get approval and win their mentor's acceptance. And that's a performance that spells disaster. Why? Because their goal will be to gain your favor rather than build a healthy marriage.

Genuineness

All of us have a built-in radar that spots phoniness. We are experts at detecting fabricated feelings and insincere intentions. We apply our own private polygraph test to every human interaction. That's why it is essential that mentors be genuine.

If you are meeting with a couple who you truthfully don't want to meet with, you have no business mentoring them. Quite simply, it won't work. They will pick up on your feeling no matter how great your acting is, and the relationship will do more harm than good.

You can fake some things, but you can't fake genuineness. Either you sincerely want to help this couple or you are merely playing the sterile role of "mentor" — hiding behind defenses or

> *Let one who wants to move and convince others, first be convinced and moved themselves. If a person speaks with genuine earnestness the thoughts, the emotion and the actual condition of their own heart, others will listen because we all are knit together by the tie of sympathy.*
>
> THOMAS CARLYLE

facades. In other words, authenticity is something you are, not something you do.

Genuineness has been described as a lure to the heart. Jesus said, "Blessed are the pure in heart." Or, to put it another way, "Consider the mentor in whom there is no guile." When genuineness is present, a hesitant and even skeptical couple is likely to stay with you and invest energy in the mentoring process. Genuineness begets gratitude.

Empathy

The best way to avoid stepping on the toes of the couple you are mentoring is to put yourself in their shoes. It's the third essential quality for effectively mentoring. Of course, you may be thinking of it more as a skill than a quality. And you're right. In fact, we'll have much more to say about it when we get to the skills of marriage mentoring in part 3 of the book. But what we are talking about here is a personality predisposition that enables you to take the focus off yourself. It is integral to your persona.

Marriage mentoring is not a showcase for your marriage. It's not about performing for this less experienced couple or dominating the conversation with stories of your life. Far from it. Mentoring necessitates the ability to set aside your own interests to zero in on what's best for the mentorees. If you have a tough time seeing life from another person's perspective, mentoring is not for you.

The extreme example of this deficit is found in the narcissistic personality. These are people who love to hear their own voice—and think everyone else does too. They are puffed up with self-importance, never recognizing how they come off to others. Of course, we can all have twinges of this at times. But if it prevents us from seeing life from our mentorees' perspective, we will never make it as a mentor. It was Sigmund Freud who said, "Whoever loves becomes humble. Those who love have, so to speak, pawned a part of their narcissism."

Empathy lets the couple you are mentoring know you are truly interested in them. You hear their words, understand their thoughts, and sense their feelings. This does not mean you necessarily understand all that is going on for them, only that you are *working* to accurately understand. We can all learn to empathize better (and we'll show you how later), but it starts with an empathic predisposition that readily recognizes that this mentoring relationship is not just about you.

CAUTION FLAGS FOR MARRIAGE MENTORS

With this exploration of the character qualities essential for marriage mentoring under our belts, we're ready to take a good look at those thorny issues that may mean a couple isn't in the right place to be effective as mentors.

Melody and Kip were such a couple. Married eleven years, they seemed to have nearly every quality they needed to be mentors except one: they had suffered a significant financial crisis just four months earlier and were still reeling from the emotional fallout. Kip had lost his business and was looking for work; in the interim Melody had picked up some part-time employment at a daycare center. When they came to us as volunteer mentors this was an immediate caution flag. Why? Because it's difficult to invest in others when you can barely look beyond your own needs. And when we raised this issue to Melody and Kip, they quickly agreed, realizing they were volunteering more for themselves than for the couple they would be mentoring. In time, however, they got back on their financial feet and were in a far better place to mentor.

> *Do not think that love, in order to be genuine, has to be extraordinary. What we need is to love without getting tired.*
> MOTHER TERESA

So, do everyday problems disqualify a couple from being good mentors? Absolutely not. Let's start this by saying it straight: every couple, no matter how happy, has problems from time to time. In fact, *half* of all newlyweds report having "significant marital problems."[1] Having problems is not a caution flag.

That said, the intensity and frequency of some problems *can* preclude a couple from being effective mentors. According to research, here are some of the most common conditions that serve as caution flags:

- You are currently battling any kind of addiction (gambling, pornography, drugs, alcohol, etc.).
- You have uncontrollable emotional outbursts that you have not yet managed.
- You have recently suffered a significant setback (financial, emotional, etc.).
- Your marriage is not stable or is fraught with frequent conflict.
- You have suffered serious emotional wounds from some kind of abuse in your life and you are still trying to find healing.
- You are struggling with significant financial debt.

- One of you is far more motivated to become a marriage mentor than the other.
- You do not have a sense of meaning and purpose in your life.
- You are pessimistic about marriage in general.
- You avoid personal responsibility for problems in your life.
- You are not content and at peace with your life and your marriage.
- You are not living your life by submitting to biblical principles.
- You are primarily motivated to be marriage mentors to help your own marriage.
- You have been told by others that you may not be in a good place to be marriage mentors right now.

This list is by no means exhaustive. It is simply a beginning place to consider what might keep a couple—perhaps even you—from being ready to be marriage mentors.

THE BOTTOM LINE

It all comes down to being relatively healthy. As we have said in our book, *I Love You More*, your marriage can only be as healthy as the least healthy person in it. Both you and your spouse need to be in a healthy place to be effective. After all, your relationship is the most important ingredient of the mentoring process. If one of you is suffering from anything that is preventing your relationship from being as healthy as it should be, you need to give it more time.

> *The unexamined life is not worth living.*
> SOCRATES

No one expects marriage mentors to be paragons of psychological and spiritual health. But marriage mentors are models of behavior. If you do not demonstrate a relatively healthy marriage, you become part of the problem rather than the solution.

Marriage Mentoring Self-Test

In light of what you've just read in this chapter, how do you think you measure up? Complete the following self-inventory to help determine the degree to which you possess some of the traits discussed.

For each statement below, indicate the response that best identifies your beliefs and attitudes. Keep in mind that the "right" answer is the one that best expresses your thoughts at this time. Use the following code:

5 = I strongly agree
4 = I agree
3 = I am undecided
2 = I disagree
1 = I strongly disagree

1. Giving advice has little to do with good mentoring. _____

2. I can accept and respect people who disagree with me. _____

3. I can make a mistake and admit it. _____

4. I look at everybody's side of a disagreement before I make a decision. _____

5. I tend to trust my intuition even when I'm unsure of the outcome. _____

6. I don't need to see immediate and concrete results in order to know progress is occurring. _____

7. Who you are in mentoring is more important that what you do. _____

8. My presence frees others from the threat of external evaluation. _____

9. In a tense emotional situation I tend to remain calm. _____

10. I know my limits when it comes to helping others. _____

Total Score (add your answers to questions 1 – 10) _____

SCORING: _____

40 – 50   You are well on your way to being an effective mentor; take special care to maintain the qualities you have.

30 – 39   You have what it takes to be effective, but you will need to exert special attention to grooming the traits described in chapter 3.

Below 30   Seek out advice and counsel to assess your strengths and to pinpoint which characteristics you need to develop further.

COMMON PITFALLS OF BEGINNING MARRIAGE MENTORS

Anyone who has never made a mistake
has never tried anything new.
ALBERT EINSTEIN

Karl Wallenda, a great tightrope aerialist, fell to his death in 1978 while walking a seventy-five-foot high wire in downtown San Juan, Puerto Rico. Shortly after this tragedy, his wife, also an aerialist, discussed that fatal walk. She recalled that all Karl thought about for three straight months prior to his attempt was falling. It was the first time he'd ever thought about failure in his work and, from her point of view, he put all his energies into not falling rather than walking the tightrope. Karl was virtually destined to make a mistake.

The marriage mentor who focuses more on his or her potential for failure than on success is, like Karl Wallenda, also likely to fall. The novice marriage mentor is especially tempted to invest a disproportionate amount of time and energy in trying to avoid mistakes instead of focusing on what it takes to be effective. Do you have a secret fear of making a mentoring blunder? If so, you are not alone. In this chapter we attempt to alleviate this kind of anxiety by turning our attention to some of the most common mistakes the beginning marriage mentor makes. The goal is to help you become aware of these pitfalls, avoid them, and put your energy into becoming the most effective marriage mentor you can be.

The following is not an exhaustive list of blunders made by beginning mentors, nor is it a catalog of the worst possible errors. Rather, it represents some of the most common mistakes made by those just starting out as marriage mentors. We have trained hundreds, if not thousands, of mentor couples and from this experience we present this list to stimulate your thinking and heighten your awareness so you can sidestep these potential pitfalls.[1]

PREMATURE PROBLEM SOLVING

Like a complex puzzle with interlocking pieces, another couple's struggle cannot normally be understood and "solved" in a brief amount of time. A problem that has in some cases been escalating for years cannot be overcome in minutes. Trying to solve a problem before it is fully understood, however, is one of the most common marriage mentoring mistakes.

Monty and Vivian revealed in their very first meeting with their mentor couple that whenever they have a conflict, Vivian leaves the house to stay with her sister across town. This infuriates Monty who sees her as not even willing to try and resolve the issue. In a couple of days, without saying anything, Vivian moves back in and goes on with life and marriage as if the incident never happened.

> *An error doesn't become a mistake until you refuse to correct it.*
> ORLANDO A. BATTISTA

Upon hearing this, Monty and Vivian's eager marriage mentors jumped right in to explain how destructive this pattern can be. "If you run from your problems, Vivian, you'll never resolve them—you'll create untold loose ends that eat away at your marriage. You've got to hang in there and discuss the issue." With that, Vivian broke into tears and walked away from the meeting.

"What did we say?"

"That's exactly what she does to me," replied Monty.

These mentors may have had good intentions, but their premature problem-solving prevented the true reason for Vivian's behavior from being unearthed. Vivian's real problem was not her avoidance of the issues, but the terrible abuse she suffered from her father. Her current coping strategy was directly related to how she was treated as a child. And neither Monty nor her mentors were taking the time to discover this.

A seasoned marriage mentor knows it is normally not easy to identify clearly and quickly any underlying issues that may be impacting a couple. These take time to make their way to the surface. That's why wise mentors major on listening before trying to solve problems.

SETTING LIMITS

In an effort to be understanding and compassionate, most beginning mentors have difficulty setting their own personal limits—dealing appropriately with such issues as repeated calls, for example, or missed appointments.

Eager to be the best mentors they could be, in the early stages of mentoring their first couple Calvin and Ruby began to get phone calls—lots of them. Their couple called during the day, while Calvin was at work. They phoned late at night when Calvin and Ruby were in bed. On top of that, this couple emailed both Calvin and Ruby routinely. Not wanting to disappoint their mentorees, Calvin and Ruby never set boundaries on these numerous contacts and they were, unwittingly, creating a very dependent relationship.

Most mentorees do not do this, by the way, but if you have a situation requiring some boundary setting, all it generally takes is a brief discussion. For example, Calvin and Ruby might say, "We want to be accessible to you two and we love it that you feel so comfortable connecting with us. But we want you to rely on yourselves more than you are doing right now. So, in the weeks ahead, let's make the phone calls and emails more of a rarity. Let's limit contacts to just one call or email per week and see how that goes. Okay? In fact, why don't you keep track of the times you're tempted to contact us and then make a note of what happened when you didn't and we'll talk about that at our next meeting."

Another potential problem area is the amount of time you spend with mentorees when you meet. Some couples you mentor may attempt to test the limits by continuing to talk past the agreed upon ending time. Of course, there may be occasions when this is justifiable. But if you continually go past the set time, this may begin to raise questions in their minds.[2] Mentorees will wonder if you are strong enough to be their mentors if you can't handle their ramblings. Do not be afraid to set limits and courteously hold to them. It's good for your mentorees to see this kind of boundary setting modeled in your own marriage.

FEAR OF SILENCE

The inexperienced mentor is often afraid of silence. The compulsion to say something during an awkward silence is natural and part of the human need to fill the gaps of everyday conversation. In mentoring, however, silence is not a sign that you need to say something. Silence does not mean that something has gone wrong. When the experienced mentor senses that the "wheels of thought and feeling" are turning, he or she gives time for the couple to reflect and contemplate. The effective marriage mentor allows this process to happen without interruption. A nervous mentor who gets anxious during silence, on the other hand, will derail a train of thought by interrupting the productive silence.

Many couples have difficulty expressing themselves on sensitive subjects such as sexuality, financial mismanagement, and in-law relationships, to name a few. Interrupting them before they have finished what they are trying to say is degrading. The effective mentor rehearses what he or she is going to say next, but holds it in check until the mentorees have fully completed the momentary struggle of thinking and talking about something that probably makes them feel very vulnerable.

There are times, of course, when silence is not productive. Some couples, for example, may be socially anxious and, for this reason, they may be unable to express themselves easily. Naive about how mentoring works, other couples may expect you to do all of the talking. But more often, silence works to a positive purpose. Some of mentoring's most positive moments occur during periods of quiet contemplation. The inexperienced mentor needs to remember that it takes some couples much longer to incorporate what you have said than it does the time it took you to say it. So become comfortable with silence and learn to maintain eye contact with your couples, nodding your head as a nonverbal expression of listening and understanding (we'll show you how in part 3).

INTERROGATION

By relying too heavily on asking questions, the inexperienced mentor may cause some couples to feel interrogated rather than understood. Interrogation and mentoring are obviously not synonymous. Little relational help takes place during an inquisition. The mentor-in-training, therefore, needs to learn to refrain from subjecting couples to a barrage of questions. Excessive probing can make them feel beleaguered, and eventually they may clam up.

It is important to understand that good information can be obtained without interrogation. In response to a wife who says, "My husband was angry at me for most of the afternoon," numerous questions could follow: How often does your husband become angry? What does he do when he is angry? How does that make you feel? However, a mentor can obtain much of this information and more by saying something to the effect, "I get the impression you have experienced your husband's anger more than once." An open-ended statement like this lets mentorees know they are understood and invites further disclosure without the risk of putting them on the spot.

The point is, it's possible for the skilled marriage mentor to elicit information without a series of threatening questions. When you actively try to understand another couple's experiences, this helps that couple open up. Relevant information then becomes more readily accessible, and a stronger mentoring alliance is built.

IMPATIENCE

Every marriage mentor watches with hope for signs of progress. Every mentor wants the couple they are with to improve and grow as soon and as much as possible. Impatience among the inexperienced mentor shows up in an eagerness to push unprepared couples into a better place before their time has come. Although "aha" moments happen in mentoring, most improvement is gradual, often slow. Gradual change is not an indicator of poor mentoring. Transformation in the mind takes time. A couple who is grieving the loss of one of their parents, for example, cannot be forced to "snap out of it." Nor can a person struggling with excessive spending be expected to quickly reverse habits that have been a long time building.

> *Every great mistake has a halfway moment, a split second when it can be recalled and perhaps remedied.*
> PEARL S. BUCK

Tony had a tough time with this. As a beginning mentor, he was eager to see his mentorees whip their rebellious teenage son into shape. "Are you disciplining him the way we talked about? If he's still acting out, it's only because you're allowing it. You've got to keep on him." Tony was beginning to sound more like a drill sergeant than a mentor. And his mentorees were losing their patience with his impatience. They quit.

Why? Because mentorees who are rushed into making rapid changes will be set up for further failure. Being pushed to show signs of improvement too soon may result in extreme defensiveness or a premature termination of mentoring altogether. For this reason you must be sensitive to issues of personal impatience, especially if you are an aggressive problem solver. Couples cannot and will not make dramatic changes quickly. Nor should they. So take your time.

MORALIZING

Mentors are never required to compromise their convictions, to relinquish the beliefs, values, and morals that are their own. Nevertheless, regardless of your couple's behaviors, you must refrain from passing judgments on the personhood of either one of them as human beings. A primary goal of mentoring is not to condemn, but to understand. This is what will give you the credibility, if not the right, to explore more constructive or biblically sound alternatives.

Understanding, of course, does not condone behavior; it does not mean the mentor becomes amoral. Not by a long shot. Say you are mentoring an engaged couple and you learn they are cohabiting. Immediately, you want to tell them there is a better way. A godly way. But bite your tongue for a bit. Take time to understand how they came to this decision. What's behind it? Get inside their heads to genuinely understand. In time you can explore whether they considered the ramifications of their choice. Eventually, you can talk to them about the lifestyle that God provides and how it will positively impact their marriage for the long haul. You may eventually point them to church policy or what-have-you. But be slow to pass moral judgment as marriage mentors. Earn the right to intervene.

Couples are rarely helped by a moralizing marriage mentor. In fact, in the majority of situations where moral judgment is declared, the probability of healthy change diminishes significantly. "When you criticize me," Carl Rogers once said, "I intuitively dig in to defend myself. However, when you accept me like I am, I suddenly find I am willing to change."[3] While holding firm to personal convictions, the effective mentor does not mistake preaching for mentoring. When a marriage mentor cannot seem to refrain from personal judgment, referral to another marriage mentor couple should be explored. And the marriage mentor should examine what lies behind the judgmental spirit before entering another mentoring relationship.

RELUCTANCE TO REFER

No mentor is expected to work with all the potential mentorees he or she encounters. The beginning marriage mentor must learn, early on, that referral to another marriage mentor, a pastor, or a counselor is a part of doing good marriage mentoring work.

If for any reason—shortage of time, a red flag (which we explore in appendix 8), lack of experience or skill, or even the capacity to be emotionally present—a mentor is unable to meet a couple's needs, referral is not only a necessity but an ethical obligation.

Careful referral involves more than giving couples the name of somebody to contact, however. You need to explain to the couple why they need to consult with someone else. Be direct and honest. Guide them in the process. You may even have them make the call with you present if they would appreciate that. And to protect against abandonment, you should follow up on the referral to determine whether or not the appropriate connection was made. Of course, a referral like this is typically very rare in marriage mentoring, but as it is such an important issue it deserves mentioning at this stage.

A FINAL THOUGHT ON MAKING MISTAKES

Fear of failure is one of the greatest obstacles that confronts the inexperienced marriage mentor. Every mentor, regardless of experience and training, will make mistakes. So be patient with yourself as you gain marriage mentoring momentum.

I (Leslie) can't help thinking about a fledgling mentor couple we first met more than eight years ago. John and Rhonda came into my office one day because they had made a "blunder."

"What happened?" I asked.

"Our mentorees asked us about how they could get out of financial debt," said Rhonda sheepishly, "and we told them as long as they could pay their credit card balance they weren't really in debt."

They went on to tell us how guilty they felt, how they've never been good with their own finances, and how they didn't deserve to be mentoring others. "I knew this was wrong," said John, "but we felt like we had to tell them something."

Eight years later, we still laugh with John and Rhonda about this. And nobody laughs louder than they do. Today, they are one of the best marriage mentor couples we know (and they've also climbed out of their own credit card debt). And it's all because they didn't quit after making mistakes.

Consider the genius inventor Thomas Edison, who was one day faced with two dejected assistants telling him, "We've just completed our seven hundredth experiment and we still don't have a light bulb. We have failed." But Edison did not agree. "We haven't failed," he said. "We now know seven hundred things not to do. We are becoming experts."

Edison's wisdom applies to beginning mentors. Each "mistake" you may make brings you one step closer to being a better marriage mentor. Mentoring is serious business. What you do as a marriage mentor can make a significant difference in the lives of other couples. For this reason you can accept any anxieties you may have about it as normal. As you log more experience and go through the training modules we provide you with in part 3, your confidence will be bolstered.

CHAPTER 4

THE BOOMERANG EFFECT OF MARRIAGE MENTORING

People learn while they teach.

SENECA

"I don't know how much we helped Doug and Susan," Joan told us, "but *we* sure got a lot out of it." Joan laughed as she was telling us about being a marriage mentor couple along with her husband of eighteen years, Larry. "Helping a young couple seemed to spark a lot of things in our own marriage that we had neglected," Larry added. Joan and Larry agreed that the benefits of being marriage mentors went both ways — to mentorees, of course, but also to mentors.

The report Joan and Larry were relaying to us has been repeated time and again with the marriage mentors we have observed. Almost mystically, something wonderful happens when a more mature couple reaches out to a new couple. We call it the boomerang effect. By helping another couple form and live out their dreams, one's own dreams for marriage are reawakened and fulfilled. It's true whether you are working with newlyweds, a couple having their first baby, or a couple overcoming a major life jolt. The benefits are immense.

C. S. Lewis had a friend, Charles Williams, who warned in his book *The Place of the Lion*: "No mind is so good that it does not need another mind to counter and equal it." The same warning is true for marriage mentors. If you will allow the process of mentoring to do good in your own marriage, if you will be receptive to the two-way process, the blessing you find in mentoring will be doubled.

51

WHAT MENTORING WILL DO FOR YOU

As an effective mentor couple, you will eventually recognize how much you receive from the couple you mentor. Because you have taken the time to be present with a couple working through various questions, your own "answers" will become clearer. The wisdom of your mentorees, perhaps so different from your own, will complement and clarify your own understanding of marriage. You will find that the ones you are mentoring will become, in some ways, your teachers, *your* mentors.

You will also be refreshed by this relationship. Mentoring will rejuvenate your marriage with the energy of youth. Almost by osmosis, the excitement of a blooming marriage in the couple you care about will begin to rub off on you. Simply being around their energetic spirits will revive and rejuvenate your marriage.

And perhaps the most common aspect of the boomerang effect we discover is satisfaction. As mentors, you will enjoy the satisfaction of work well done. When a married couple successfully works on any project together—whether wallpapering a room, raking autumn leaves, or planting a garden—a sense of satisfaction results. And when a couple works on a project that has lasting value, even eternal significance—such as marriage mentoring—there is an overwhelming sense of having done good.

The diversity of marriage mentoring styles and the complexity of mentoree couples prevent a detailed listing of exactly how your mentoring experience will be mutually beneficial. But we know it will.

> *The greatest good you can do for another is not just to share your riches, but to reveal to him his own.*
>
> BENJAMIN DISRAELI

In his book *The Lives of the Desert Fathers*, Norman Russell tells a story about an ascetic who lived alone in the desert. But eventually he returned to the life of community after a dream in which an angel advised him: "God has accepted your repentance and has had mercy on you. In the future take care that you are not deceived. The brethren to whom you gave spiritual counsel will come to console you, and they will bring you gifts. Welcome them, eat with them and always give thanks to God for them."

As marriage mentors, the awareness that your mentorees bring you gifts and that you need to welcome these gifts and give thanks to God for them is one of the most important aspects of your mentoring.

WHAT OTHER MENTORS HAVE SAID

To encourage you in how you might experience the boomerang effect of marriage mentoring, we want to share with you just a sampling of what some of the mentors we have known said about the experience:

> It never occurred to us that mentoring another couple would actually strengthen our own relationship, but that's exactly what it did. Something about working as a team to help another couple brought us closer. So much so, that we haven't stopped mentoring since we took on our first couple three years ago. And every couple we mentor unknowingly supplies us with a unique gift for our own marriage.
>
> DAVID AND TAMMY, MARRIED 19 YEARS

> Mentoring another couple causes us to talk about our own marriage more than we ever have before. We are enjoying some of the best conversations we've ever had because of it.
>
> ANTHONY AND REBECCA, MARRIED 41 YEARS

> We were insecure about being mentors when we first started, but now that we are mentoring our third newlywed couple most of our anxiety has been replaced by an overwhelming sense of blessing. We see ourselves in these couples and we almost always feel more romantic and closer together when we are mentoring.
>
> JAY AND FELICIA, MARRIED 9 YEARS

> We've been mentoring couples on the brink of divorce and since we've been there ourselves, we have a good idea of what they are experiencing. This experience renews our own commitment and makes us count our blessings, never taking our personal progress for granted.
>
> BRIAN AND DEE, MARRIED 38 YEARS

> We also think of our mentoring session like a date night. Not that we aren't doing serious work, but we typically feel like the batteries in our own marriage were recharged as a result of our mentoring.
>
> JERRY AND TAYLOR, MARRIED 22 YEARS

You see, the boomerang effect of marriage mentoring is significant. When you do good for another couple you're almost sure to receive more good in return.

OUR PRAYER FOR YOU

As we mentioned earlier, the term *mentor* comes from the ancient Greek epic, *The Odyssey*, whose hero Odysseus appointed his elderly friend and adviser Mentor as his son's guardian before going off to war. In a very real sense you will become the guardians of the marriages you mentor.

So our prayer for you is that your mentorees would dare to speak of joys and sorrows, entrusting you with their hearts, and that in return you would guard their marriage as you rely on God's strength and grace to guard yours.

Successful people turn everyone who can help them into sometime mentors!

JOHN CROSBY

PART TWO

The MARRIAGE MENTORING TRIAD

We loved you so much
that we were delighted to share with you
not only the gospel of God but our lives as well.

1 THESSALONIANS 2:8

The marriage mentoring triad can be easily depicted as a triangle with three major emphases. Most people can quickly and intuitively grasp the areas where mentors can be useful.

MAXIMIZING
Deepening and enriching
stable marriages

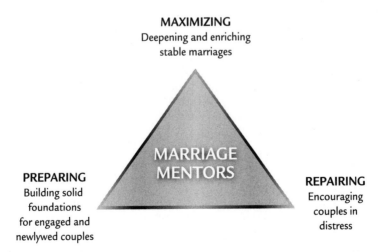

MARRIAGE MENTORS

PREPARING
Building solid
foundations
for engaged and
newlywed couples

REPAIRING
Encouraging
couples in
distress

CHAPTER 5

PREPARING:
MENTORING ENGAGED
AND NEWLYWED COUPLES

"Come to the edge," he said. They said, "We are afraid."
"Come to the edge," he said. They came.
He pushed them ... and they flew.
GUILLAUME APOLLINAIRE

The first sentence of Chaim Potok's novel, *In the Beginning*, reads " ... all beginnings are hard." Potok elaborates through his main character, David, who describes how one evening when he was nine years old, he burst into tears because a passage of a Bible commentary had proved too difficult for him to understand. David's mentor welcomed him warmly to his apartment and spoke in a gentle voice: "Be patient, David, beginnings are hard; you cannot swallow all the world at one time."

The same is true for marriage. So often we think of a marriage ceremony as the culmination of a courtship process. But in reality, it is only a beginning. It marks the start of lifelong love, offering newlyweds the opportunity to cultivate positive habits right from the start that will pay off for them down through the decades.

The engagement period and newlywed months for a couple offer an especially important opportunity for marriage mentors. In fact, in working with well over one thousand newlyweds over the years, we've come to believe that marriage mentoring is every bit as important as premarital counseling, maybe more so. A recent study at Florida State University revealed that engaged couples who are working with a mentor couple are more likely to make informed decisions when choosing a marriage partner, are more realistic in their expectations about married life, are more aware of personal differences that may impact their relationship, and better acquire communication and conflict resolution skills.[1]

More than at any other time in their married life, this window of opportunity can be the point at which they develop healthy habits that last a lifetime. Marriage mentors, at this juncture, have the opportunity to literally prevent untold sorrow and suffering for a novice couple by equipping them for the inevitable bends in the road that they can't even imagine at this stage.

> *The success of a marriage comes not in finding the "right" person, but in the ability of both partners to adjust to the real person they inevitably realize they married.*
> JOHN FISHER

The high rate of marital distress and divorce within the first few years of marriage is well documented.[2] Approximately 25 percent of marital disruptions occur before the third anniversary. Thirty-two percent of couples who separate or divorce do so by the fourth year of marriage.[3]

So in this chapter we give our attention to these couples just starting out. We begin with an exploration of the common issues faced by couples at this stage. We'll provide a list of essential tasks to help them accomplish and explore in depth the areas where they are most likely to need your help. We conclude the chapter by revealing a secret wedding gift you can impart to your mentorees, a gift that will keep on giving the rest of their days.

Before going further, we should also mention that working with newlyweds and engaged couples is one of our deepest concerns. We are passionate about turning around the divorce rate and we know that this goal hinges on helping couples get started right. In fact, for nearly two decades we have made it our job to study everything we can find to help engaged and newlywed couples get off on the right foot. And ten years ago we wrote a book and developed a comprehensive group of materials on the subject (including workbooks and a DVD curriculum), which has proved popular ever since. In fact, we recently updated this entire resource. Entitled *Saving Your Marriage Before It Starts*, it has helped over half a million couples build their house with solid foundations. You can find out more about these materials, and those for couples starting a second marriage (*Saving Your Second Marriage Before It Starts*) in appendix 3. Of course, if you are mentoring engaged and newlywed couples you can use other programs that may be available, but we are obviously most familiar with the one we developed.

PREDICTABLE ISSUES FOR ENGAGED AND NEWLYWED COUPLES

Every couple, regardless of how well prepared or how long they have dated before getting married, runs into some predictable issues. And every marriage mentor who is focusing on this stage must be well versed in these areas. Why? Because newly married couples need to succeed in a number of predictable areas early on to ensure a successful start. Failure to do so contributes to what researchers have identified as the "duration of marriage effect"—the tendency for marital satisfaction to decrease over time. These typical tasks include the following:

- establishing marital roles and responsibilities through negotiation and adjusting expectations, which we explore further below
- providing emotional fulfillment and support for each other by learning how to give and receive love and affection
- adjusting personal habits such as sleep patterns, spending behavior, and so on
- negotiating gender roles that reflect individual personalities, skills, needs, interests, values, and equity
- making sexual adjustments with each other by learning how to physically discover mutual pleasure and satisfaction
- establishing family and employment priorities by learning to balance and negotiate
- developing effective communication skills that allow resolution to conflicts
- managing budgetary and financial matters
- establishing relationships with extended family and managing to set boundaries between their marriage and family of origin
- participating in the larger community by making friends with other married couples and being involved in the community

Each of the above tasks can obviously be given a boost, when needed, through marriage mentoring. Some tasks will come easily and naturally for the couple. Others may need more direct input from you. The point is not to approach this as a punch list with your couple, but to simply be aware of these specific issues in the course of your work with them.

Next we'll look in depth at several vital areas which tend to cause the greatest consternation for newly married couples: establishing roles, dealing with conflict, handling money, developing sexual intimacy, relating with in-laws, and celebrating holidays and creating family traditions.

Establishing Marital Roles

Every new couple comes into a marriage with what we call "unconscious role expectations." These are powerful expectations held by a bride and groom of exactly what a loving husband or wife should say, do, and think. They are unconscious because they have slowly been developing without effort over the years. You see, unconscious role expectations aren't intentional; they come primarily from the homes we grew up in. In fact, we often say that our family of origin was our "university of relationships." As a young girl, whenever I (Leslie) saw my mom and dad in the car, Dad would open my mother's car door when we arrived at our destination. I never gave it much thought. I suppose I always assumed that's something husbands simply do. Well, it didn't take me long to learn that in my marriage to Les this was a myth. Not every husband does this. At least not mine!

It's true. I (Les) hardly ever saw my dad do that for my mom. They have a great marriage, but this was not one of their role expectations. Consequently, it's not one of mine.

Did this impact our early years of marriage? You bet. Does it still impact our marriage? A little. You see, these role expectations—whether they are fulfilled or not—tend to stay with us. That's why it's important to help newlyweds make their unconscious role expectations more conscious. In our *Saving Your Marriage Before It Starts* book and workbooks we provide an exercise that is ideal for doing just that. It's called, not surprisingly, "Making Your Roles Conscious" and it's very simple and often fun to do with couples.

Here's how it works: We list about twenty-five roles such as providing income, doing yard work, handling finances, grocery shopping, planning vacations, disciplining children, fixing things around the house, and so on. And for each role we have the couple determine who did that in their family of origin. Was it their mother or father or both? Then we have them determine who they expect to fulfill this role in their new marriage.

Most new couples love doing this exercise and it's almost always an eye-opener. In fact, we often use it as one of the first exercises we do with engaged or newlywed couples whom we are mentoring.

Managing Conflict

Most newlyweds will encounter a serious conflict sometime in the first few months of marriage. In fact, it's not unusual for a fight to erupt very early on. After all, this is the biggest life transition these two individuals are ever likely to make. Add to it the pressure of planning a wedding and all the idealism that goes along with it and you have fertile ground for conflict.

Scripture underscores this in James 4:1–2 where it asks: "What causes fights and quarrels among you? Don't they come from your desires that battle within you? You want something but don't get it." As you mentor newlyweds on resolving conflict, this is an important point to keep in mind: conflict begins when one person doesn't get something they want. It's a simple point but remembering where conflict comes from is often the first step to resolving it. Of course, there's more to it than that.

Granted, a newlywed couple may have learned some conflict resolution skills prior to marriage but putting those skills into practice can be a challenge. That's where you come in. A marriage mentor couple can become an extremely valuable asset to a newlywed couple trying to practice what they've already learned to do.

"Shortly after our first blowup," a new wife confided in us, "David and I both wondered if we had made a huge mistake. Maybe we married the wrong person." She went on to tell us that it was their mentor couple who put the fight into perspective for them and helped them see that it wasn't unusual or cause for serious concern.

The goal of marriage is not to avoid conflict. Not by a long shot. Conflict — if handled correctly — can help build a stronger marriage. We have said it at least a hundred times: *Conflict is the price smart couples pay for a deepening sense of intimacy.* Without conflict it is difficult to peel away the superficial layers of a relationship and discover who we really are. When Ruth Graham was asked if she and her famous evangelist husband, Billy, ever fight, she said, "I hope so. Otherwise we would have no differences, and life would be pretty boring."

No matter how deeply a man and woman love each other, they *will* encounter conflict. It is a natural component of every healthy marriage. So help your mentorees to avoid burying their differences. After all, repressed conflict has a high rate of resurrection. If something is bothering one of them it is always best to have them put it out on the table and discuss it.

And if you're looking for a few tips on guiding them to fight fair, here you go. First, teach them to plan a peace conference. In other words, they can set a time to discuss what's bothering them. It is critically important to talk about it face-to-face. Next, encourage a win-win attitude. In other words, teach them to understand their partner before "proving their case."

Too many spouses become instant attorneys when it comes to marital conflict, convincing an invisible jury (maybe even their mentors) that they have been treated unjustly and that their partner should be found guilty. Don't fall for this fallacy. The goal of fighting fair is not to prove your partner wrong so that you win, but to understand one another so you both win.

This leads to another tip: Attack the problem, not the person. If you accuse your spouse of always making you late, she is probably not going to say, "Oh, you're right. I'll be different from now on." She is likely to tell you that you only make it worse by pressuring her, or that you are too impatient, or a hundred other reasons why she is not at fault. The key is to separate the problem from the partner.

We often find it helpful to teach newlyweds how to rank the depth of their disagreement. In fact, we do this with a tangible rating system of 1 to 10, where 1 means "I'm not enthusiastic, but it's no big deal to me" and 10 means "Over my dead body!" You can actually download what we call a "conflict card" from our www.RealRelationships.com website, then print off a couple and bring them to your mentoring meeting. Whether your mentorees are arguing about how long the in-laws stay for Christmas or what color to paint the kitchen, this simple ranking method can go a long way in helping them reach a compromise.

Of course, sometimes a deep conflict requires more than compromise; it requires repentance and forgiveness (both granting and receiving it) and reconciliation. These are all key to growing through conflict and they are the heart of the gospel. Consider just a few of the numerous Scriptures on the subject, including Matthew 6–7, Romans 12, 2 Corinthians 7, and Galatians 6:1.

To sum up, you want to help show your couple how they can flex and yield to one another. Scripture says, "Wisdom ... is peace-loving and courteous. It allows discussion and is willing to yield to others; it is full of mercy and good deeds. It is wholehearted and straightforward and sincere" (James 3:17 LB). If they decide to have a cooperative attitude with each other they will save themselves and their marriage much unnecessary grief.

Conflict resolution is an extremely important skill set. This doesn't mean that as a mentor you need to be an expert at it, but without even the simple guidance of a caring marriage mentor couple, some newlyweds are bound to fall into destructive patterns of fighting that may never be remedied. For this reason, managing conflict is a common and significant issue in mentoring engaged and newlywed couples.

Handling Money

Money has always provided plenty of fodder for marital discord. It is, after all, the most common source of conflict between couples. And with good reason. The dollar (or pound, or euro, or rand) serves as a weapon of independence. The person who holds the purse strings wields the power. Money also provides a battleground for disputes over responsibility and judgment. Because the results of financial decisions are often tangible, it becomes very tempting to lay blame when a money mistake is made. Money is also the catalyst for marital conflict because it so often represents the measure of personal success and self-worth—especially for men. Of course, having a certain amount of money is no guarantee of security or freedom, but believing that making more money will give us more peace of mind is a trap many couples fall into. And that trap causes us to give more importance to money than it deserves, thus sparking more financial fights.

> *The bonds of matrimony are like any other bonds, they mature slowly.*
> PETER DE VRIES

On a deeper level, financial issues can even be a forum for airing doubts about self-worth. A partner who is financially irresponsible, for example, may be broadcasting a message that says "Rescue me, I need your help." A spouse's reluctance to accept gifts may hide a deeper lack of trust. A new bride who goes on a spending spree every time her husband becomes cold and withdrawn may be trying to get his attention. The point is that money matters run deep in every marriage and deserve serious attention right from the start. Otherwise it's a topic that may become taboo.

"We can talk about almost anything except money." It's a statement we've heard from the majority of newlywed couples we've mentored. Money is a touchy subject. The topic sometimes brings out the worst in people. We become withdrawn, pushy, or manipulative. But it doesn't have to be that way. With your help, a new couple can cultivate the right attitude and effectively communicate about getting out of debt, spending and giving, investing, and all the rest.

A good place to start is by comparing spending styles. How did their childhoods shape their beliefs about money? How were financial decisions made in the home where each of them grew up? Were money problems discussed openly? This kind of discussion will give them empathy for each other's money style and help them move into discussing how they each approach money today. What are their spending priorities right now? Are they in sync with each other? The goal is to communicate and maybe compromise; not to evaluate and judge. So help them to avoid thinking in terms of right or wrong, and instead get them thinking only about differences. Have them put themselves in each other's shoes. A little empathy goes a long way in talking about money.

If appropriate, this area can be a good place to explore biblical wisdom with your mentorees. The Bible contains numerous secrets to financial success in marriage. And one of the best kept secrets is found in the book of Proverbs. It has to do with recognizing money's power. You see, money is very alluring and deceiving. And when our greed is seduced by money's enticement, it becomes a mistress. Paul saw this fact when he observed that "the love of money is a root of all kinds of evils" (1 Timothy 6:10).

Every marriage must protect itself against greed and self-centered consumerism. And one of the best ways to do this is to give money away. Some newlyweds will immediately bristle at this. And looking at their bank account you can easily understand why. But Proverbs 3:9 urges us to do so: "Honor the LORD with your wealth, with the firstfruits of all your crops." The point for mentorees to understand is that God has given us all we have. And by giving a portion of what he has given us back to him, we free ourselves from its tyranny.

The Bible calls us to "profane" the god of money by giving it away. And to do that, we must take Christ's famous exhortation and apply it to our checkbooks: "Where your treasure is," Jesus said, "there your heart will be also" (Matthew 6:21). The point is that money holds invisible spiritual powers that can tear at the fabric of your marriage. That's why it is critically important to protect yourself against it.

That said, you want to steer clear of giving a Sunday school lesson as a marriage mentor couple. That's not your role. And you need to be sensitive to the couple you are mentoring. They may not be in a place to hear this kind of message. Tread softly. Be gentle.

Enjoying Physical Intimacy

Okay, we can almost feel you tensing up as you read this heading. And we've heard plenty of new mentors say, "We'll talk about anything with our mentorees but sex!" We understand. After all, what could be more personal? But at the same time what subject could be more helpful for newlyweds to discuss with mentors—a seasoned couple who isn't related to them? You are in a unique relationship with this couple and this topic is one in which you might be particularly helpful.

So let us give you a little advice on how to talk about sex without being nervous. Why? Because even if this is a subject you want to avoid, your mentorees may very well bring it up themselves. And you don't want to look like a deer caught in headlights if a new bride says, "So, is it normal for intercourse to hurt?" Or a new groom says, "How many times each night are we supposed to have sex?"

By far the most common question from new couples has to do with differing sexual desires. It is not unusual for couples to feel out of sync when it comes to the desire and frequency of lovemaking. Differing desires seem to be part of many marriages. And more often than not, it is the woman who may lack interest. Why? There are a couple primary and universal reasons for this.

First, women don't have testosterone. The hormone testosterone stimulates sexual drive and circulates at far higher levels in the bloodstream of men than women. The result is that men think about sex more often than women. And second, girls are traditionally taught to be sexually reserved. This modesty about sexual exposure and aggressiveness often extends into the marriage relationship. As mentors, we've often heard from couples where the woman doesn't even want her new husband to see her without clothes. Of course, this can discourage a young groom who had ideas of his wife doing most things around the house naked!

So when the issue of sex is looming large, don't ignore it. Put the emphasis back on the newlyweds. Help them discuss it with each other. Ask them for their opinions before you give them any advice. If a new husband asks you why his bride doesn't initiate sex, suggest that he ask her right there in front of you. Empathize with each spouse. Be patient as they process. Then, if appropriate, you can tell them what you know. You can make suggestions. You can reveal what has worked (and what hasn't) for the two of you.

Of course, you are bound to get questions of a sexual nature that you may not know how to handle. In that case, turn to the sex experts. For us, that's Dr. Cliff and Joyce Penner, whose terrific book *Getting Your Sex Life Off to a Great Start* dispels many myths, explores biblical passion, and helps husbands and wives understand each other's bodies. We keep a couple copies of this resource handy for our mentorees and you may want to as well. But whether it's this resource or another, we've found it helpful to have a practical tool we can give to newlyweds.

Dealing with In-Laws

Someone once observed that Adam and Eve got along as well as they did because neither had any in-laws to worry about. Maybe so, but they still had their problems. One can only imagine that having in-laws might have compounded them. Or would they have lightened their load? Perhaps their seemingly impossible babysitting problem would have been solved. Who knows?

It seems some newlywed couples couldn't be happier with their in-laws, while other couples feel that their in-laws are the source of most of their problems. Couples in the latter group are not alone. Experts believe that three-quarters of all married couples have problems with their in-laws.

Some of the most common in-law problems include keeping a son-in-law or daughter-in-law at a distance, giving them the cold shoulder and treating them as a person who has invaded the family or is not good enough for their son or daughter. Another common in-law issue involves gift-giving with strings attached. This occurs when the parents offer some kind of help (monetary or otherwise) and then treat it as a license to tell the newlyweds exactly how to use it. Of course, criticism is also a major in-law complaint by couples. Some in-laws constantly critique each and every choice a couple makes.

An extreme in-law problem appears when parents intrude. They may smother and hover over the marriage without making room for the couple to have privacy, dabbling in things that aren't their business. Winston Churchill's "darling Clementine" learned early that she had married not just her husband but his strong-willed mother as well. When she and Winston returned from their honeymoon, the young bride discovered that Lady Randolph Churchill had completely redecorated the couple's new home in a style far fancier than Clementine had planned.

As marriage mentors to newlyweds, in-law issues can be dicey. You obviously want to avoid choosing sides. You don't want to pass judgment on either set of their parents. What you *do* want is to be a sounding board. You want to listen. And you may want to eventually talk about your own in-law issues if that might be useful. The point is to be aware that in-law issues are bound to be brought up. And if they aren't, it's a good topic for you to initiate.

Trying to sort out what kind of relationship to have with one's own family and a spouse's family can be a challenge. But resolving this issue is vital to the health of a marriage. The goal for newlyweds, of course, is to shift allegiances away from family and friends and focus their allegiances on each other.

Recently we mentored a newlywed couple where the husband's parents were being particularly pushy. They would often drop in unannounced, make lots of suggestions on how to arrange the furniture, where the couple should do their grocery shopping, when they should plan on having children. In other words, these were invasive in-laws!

In the course of our conversations with them, we suggested that they take a look at what they were doing that gave his parents the "right" to meddle in their marriage. "What do you mean?" they asked. We went on to explain that they might be receiving something, maybe financial help,

Keeping In-Laws from Becoming Out-Laws

Admit the potential for problems. The first step in building a better relationship is to recognize the possibility of hitting some turbulence. If you try to ignore it, the problems will only become bigger.

Talk about your perspectives. Once you admit the potential for problems to yourself, share your differing perspectives with each other—just the two of you, in a calm and compassionate atmosphere.

Make plans early. If both families are expecting you to join them for the holidays, for example, make advanced plans. This gives everyone time to adjust their feelings.

Give and take without being finicky. You will only complicate your problem if you do not avail yourself of old-fashioned flexibility. Maybe this year will be spent with your partner's family and next year with yours. The point is to be open to suggestions and compromise.

Be careful how you compromise. Sometimes couples get caught in the trap of trying to please everyone but themselves. It is important that you focus on making your vacation or holiday special for the two of you and not just your families.

Be loyal to each other. If it is not already crystal clear, make sure your parents know that—even though you love them dearly—your marriage is your priority.

Be positive when things turn negative. Balancing both families is never easy. Difficult circumstances are bound to occur. So decide in advance to adjust to circumstances beyond your control with a positive outlook. This single step may be the most important key to keeping in-laws from becoming out-laws.

that made his parents feel like they had every right to intrude in their marriage.

Our mentorees immediately looked at each other with knowing eyes and said simultaneously, "The car." They proceeded to tell us that his parents sacrificed to give them a brand-new vehicle for a wedding gift. That insight—that the car seemed to unknowingly come with a major string attached—was a breakthrough moment. They met with his parents the next day to gently discuss the implication of their generous gift and the problem began to ease. In fact, in this instance, we actually role-played with them how the conversation might go. This is a technique for marriage mentors that is often effective.

Celebrating Holidays and Creating Family Traditions

How a couple celebrates Thanksgiving, Christmas, New Year's, and so on, during their first year or two of marriage often sets a pattern for all the holidays that follow. Typically, these holidays have been spent with their families and they never had to blend new and different traditions into their own. And too often, newlyweds do not deliberately consider how to prepare for holidays as a couple. If they aren't intentional, holidays can become a tremendous source of stress and lead to unnecessary conflict.

So what can you do as marriage mentors to help? Plenty. All you have to do is bring up the topic and the problems often begin to resolve themselves. Why? Because you're helping them talk about this subject before it becomes an "issue." The best place to begin is by asking them what they expect their Thanksgiving and Christmas to be like. In the course of this discussion, you might talk to them about your own first Christmas and how personal expectations differed. You might share with them how you resolved the matter and how you eventually developed your own traditions together.

You might also ask them about how birthdays are to be celebrated. One mentoree couple we met with told how her first birthday as a wife was a disaster. You see, in her home growing up, a birthday was a major occasion. She was one of two sisters and the family really celebrated with special outings and surprises all week long. But in her husband's home, you got a card and, if you were lucky, a gift certificate.

Exploring their family backgrounds and how they shaped their holiday and birthday celebrations shed a lot of light for this couple. And it does for all mentorees. By helping them think these things through and plan ahead, your newlywed couple can set up positive patterns that will forever enrich their relationship.

DEVELOPING THE HONEYMOON HABIT

When they married eighteen months ago, Kim never would have dreamed she'd find herself complaining that her husband Steve didn't show her enough affection. "He was so attentive that he would notice if I changed a part in my hair or bought a new blouse," Kim says. But the loving words and compliments come a little less often now, and frankly, Kim misses the special attention. "He thinks I'm the one who's cooling off," she shrugs, "but I just can't get interested in sex when I feel I'm being ignored."

Kim and Steve aren't alone. The frequent expressions of affection and approval that couples give each other during the courtship and honeymoon stage can dwindle during the first few years of marriage. Let's make this perfectly clear. Contrary to the fairy tales we were weaned on, romance always runs the risk of fading. No, let us rephrase that—romance always fades. As human beings, we aren't built to maintain the high levels of feverish passion and romance experienced during the days of engagement and the honeymoon. And yet that's exactly what most couples, like Kim and Steve, expect.

> *We have been poisoned by fairy tales.*
> ANAIS NIN

Even the more mature stories of doomed love reinforce this notion. Remember the tragic twosome Romeo and Juliet? How about Lancelot and Guinevere? Rhett and Scarlett? Each snuffed out their powerful love while the heat of passion was turned up full blast. Why? Because it couldn't last. The heat of passion was never meant to. Can you imagine Romeo and Juliet as a married couple ... going off to work ... paying bills ... grocery shopping? It's almost incongruous; at least it takes a lot of the luster off their love story. The point is that all the romancing and wooing that leads up to a marriage cannot sustain it. Not in real life.

No couple can realistically expect their marriage to be a long-running cinematic fairy tale. Those couples who hold on to this faulty expectation end up drinking the "poison" of untold heartache. But, with the help of a marriage mentor couple, there is a better way.

You can help newlywed couples keep romantic love alive long after the honeymoon has ended. The secret? We call it "The Honeymoon Habit" and you instill it as a mentor couple when you help newlyweds do everything they can in their early years of marriage to establish habits of loving behavior.

A habit is a recurrent, often unconscious pattern of behavior acquired through frequent repetition. If you repeat a behavior often enough, it becomes a pattern. Eventually, you hardly give it a thought. The behavior becomes second nature. Whether it be fastening a seat belt when you get in a car or biting your fingernails to pass the time, habits shape our actions, both positive and negative. They can lead to behaviors that cultivate and nurture lasting love or they can lead to behaviors that serve as love's saboteur. Most importantly, once a habit is "set," it's next to impossible to break.

Why all this talk about habits? Because as marriage mentors to newlyweds, you have a rare opportunity to shape and determine many of the habits a newlywed couple will have for the rest of their marriage. The little things they do now—without thinking—will cut a groove in their relationship that will likely last a lifetime.

So we urge you to help the couple in your care take charge of their romantic destiny. Help them establish patterns of loving behavior that will keep romance, passion, and intimacy alive and well. In fact, here is a two-step, post-honeymoon plan that many mentors to newlyweds have found helpful.

Help Them Note the Little Things

Have you ever been bit by an elephant? Chances are you haven't. Have you ever been bit by a mosquito? Probably. It's a silly illustration, but it makes a point: little things often matter most. Especially in marriage. Too often, we think on a grand scale about romance—creating the perfect once-a-year getaway—and neglect the little opportunities that present themselves every day in marriage.

Help newlyweds consider, for example, how they greet one another when returning home from work. If they begin by making a consistent effort to reconnect with a tender touch or embrace at the end of their day, they will establish one of the most important patterns couples can have for setting a positive tone for their evening together.

"Well, of course we'll do that," they may say to you. But let them know that the vast majority of couples end up with what researchers call the "grocery list" connection: Did you pick up my dry cleaning? I'll need the car tomorrow. What's for dinner?

But they can avoid this if they intentionally enjoy a tender touch when they arrive home before getting to the nitty-gritty tasks of the day. They will create an aura of love in their home that leads to a level of fulfillment most married couples only dream about. Sure, it's a little thing, but a tender reconnection at the end of their day makes a huge difference when it becomes a habit.

Other "little things" to consider include common courtesies like saying *please* and *thank you.* Did you know that one of the first things to go in a new marriage is politeness? In some ways this reflects increasing levels of comfort. But if left unchecked, it can lead to rudeness. One study revealed that when paired with a stranger, even newlyweds were more polite to him or her than they were toward each other. If they establish a pattern of politeness now, they'll likely be even more polite on their fiftieth wedding anniversary!

> *"And they lived happily ever after" is one of the most tragic sentences in literature. It's tragic because it's a falsehood. It is a myth that has led generations to expect something from marriage that is not possible.*
>
> JOSHUA LIEVMAN

Teach Them to Make Dating a Habit

Many married couples claim they spend time together. But when you question them, you find they are spending that time running errands or meeting with other friends. There's nothing wrong with that, of course, but to keep romance alive, a couple needs to have quality time together, just the two of them, with no other agenda except to connect. Some married couples call it their date night. And that's not a bad title. After all, there is no rule that says dating ends when you get married. In fact, dating becomes as important as ever after husband and wife have said their vows and settled into being a married couple. Whatever you call it, this time needs to be scheduled—routinely and consistently.

Every Thursday evening, for example, you need to be able to count on having a date: a leisurely dinner at your favorite restaurant, window shopping downtown, a picnic at a local park, taking in a movie and ice cream, dressing up for a special event. Remind mentorees to continue enjoying the same things they enjoyed before they were married. The point of making dating a habit is to keep their marriage from falling into the doldrums of working all week and collapsing on the weekends. This toxic pattern has snuffed out the romantic flame of more couples than you can imagine. Don't let it happen to the couple you're mentoring.

By the way, as you are probably already aware, once kids enter the picture these romantic interludes become all the more essential. And if they don't establish the pattern of dating now, while they are just starting out, they are unlikely to do so when their lives become more hectic.

Over the years many couples return to the place of their first wedding trip for a second, third, or fourth honeymoon. It seems many work hard to recapture the bliss of their first few days as a couple. But a couple doesn't have to wait for an anniversary or special occasion to recreate that special time. Help the newlyweds you mentor to keep love alive by establishing daily habits of romance, passion, and intimacy. If they do, their honeymoon will become more than a memory; it can become a way of life.

CHAPTER 6

MAXIMIZING: MENTORING COUPLES FROM GOOD TO GREAT

A marriage made in heaven is one where a man and a woman
become more richly themselves together than the chances
are either of them could ever have managed to become alone.

FREDERICK BUECHNER

Sometimes the most neglected couples in a congregation are the couples who are "doing just fine." These are the couples who aren't coping with a crisis. Their children are not acting out any more than is usual. They aren't struggling financially. From every indication they are committed to each other and in love. They are good citizens and church attendees. As we said, they are doing just fine. So what's the issue?

To be frank, these good couples may be missing out on something great.

In the internationally bestselling business book *Good to Great*, Jim Collins shows his readers "why some companies make the leap ... and others don't." He reveals how close some companies come to greatness but never quite make it, while others take the daring leap to do just that. The same is true for good marriages. Some good couples move just beyond being mediocre and think that's it. But it's not. With a little insight and a little effort, they could be on the brink of greatness. They could make the leap and enjoy what only the top 10 percent of loving couples enjoy.

Our friend and colleague Dr. Doug McKinley, a Christian psychologist in Chicago, often says that the greatest enemy to a great marriage is a good marriage. And he's exactly right. That's why so few couples in a good marriage aspire to something better. They look around at other couples and realize they aren't doing too bad. *At least we don't have their problems*, they think to themselves. *We're doing okay.* And they are. But they've settled for the state they are in, and by default, they've become complacent.

But it doesn't have to be this way. A good couple can make the leap to greatness—especially when marriage mentors are involved. And so we dedicate this chapter to every mentor couple who would like to help others move from good to great, to maximize their marriage (see again the marriage mentor triad diagram on page 55).

COMMON ISSUES TO EXPLORE

What keeps most couples from moving into the upper echelons of marital satisfaction? More money? A nicer house? Expensive vacations? Better jobs? Of course not! It's the intangibles. It's the rare qualities that the majority of struggling couples don't even seem to bother with. It's the extraordinary and uncommon qualities that set them apart. Qualities like service that outweighs selfishness. And purpose that overshadows plodding. Granted, these are issues that can benefit most any couple, regardless of age or stage, but they typically don't appear on a couple's radar screen until other, more pressing needs are firmly met.

Ask any couple who is sailing along pretty well in their marriage what is keeping them from getting to the next level and more often than not, their reply will fall into one of two categories—or both. They are likely to tell you that their primary stumbling block is either the lack of time or the lack of good communication. Couples who have been married for years, with or without children, continually rank "time" and "talk" as their greatest deficits.

In this chapter we're going to explore the uncommon and often unnoticed qualities that take a couple from good to great, as well as some of the more recognizable ones. We begin with an interesting exercise and an exploration of the three most common issues related to mentoring these couples: selfishness (rather than service), plodding along (rather than living on purpose), and merely parenting (rather than parenting with pleasure). And we wrap up the chapter with some thoughts on laughter, the telltale sign of a marriage that is enjoying greatness.

Asking the Big Question

Have you ever been in a public setting, maybe at a party, and you get a smudge on your face or a piece of food on your upper lip? It happens to everyone. But not everyone will point out the problem. It's embarrassing to most people—but not your spouse. He or she will waste no time in telling you what you don't know about your appearance and how to correct it. And you'll be grateful. What you may not appreciate is when your spouse does the same thing for personal problems you'd rather not admit. "You're quick-tempered," your spouse may say. Or, "You sometimes come off as insensitive." *What?! How dare you try to tell me about myself?* When your spouse hits a tender spot you immediately put up your guard and measure your defenses. It's only natural. It goes against our grain to hear information about our dark side, the part of us we wish weren't true. But this very information is vital to the life of a good marriage.

It's taken a while for me (Leslie) to learn this lesson. Receiving feedback on my foibles is not my idea of a good time. Les, on the other hand, seems to thrive on it. More than once he has caught me off guard with a simple question: "What would make me a better husband?" The first time he asked this I thought he was joking, but he meant it. And through the years I've learned from his example, sometimes painfully so. But it is well worth it.

Let me give you a quick example. I consider myself a good listener. I've not only had advanced training in my graduate work on this skill, I am naturally predisposed to lend an ear to friends, family, almost anyone. But some time ago, I discovered something about my listening style that irritated some people—including Les. "Are you aware of how often you finish my sentences," he said, "and how often you are wrong when you do?" *What?!* "I know you are good intentioned," he continued, "but I've seen you do this a lot and it's kind of annoying." Les gave me some examples of how I put words in another's mouth to let them know I'm tracking, that I understand what they are saying. "I don't like it when you jump to conclusions about what I'm saying; it sometimes comes off like you are getting impatient with me." He was right. As tough as it was to hear, Les showed me a part of myself and helped me change my behavior, as well as my marriage, for the better.

This idea gave birth to a five- to ten-minute exercise we often teach marriage mentorees who want to go from good to great in their relationship. We call it The Big Question, which is simply, "What would make me a better spouse this week?"

It's as easy as asking couples to write on a piece of paper one thing their spouse could do right now to be a better marriage partner. On the same paper they should write one thing their spouse is already doing that makes them a good marriage partner plus a concrete example from the past week that backs up their point. As they share what they have written, it not only gives each partner a nice boost but also something to work on in the days ahead. It's a terrific tool for moving a marriage from good to great.

Moving from Plodding to Purpose

"Let your eyes look straight ahead, fix your gaze directly before you. Make level paths for your feet and take only ways that are firm," says Proverbs 4:25–26. That's good counsel—whether you are trying to find your way through city streets or charting the course of your marriage. Of course, no marriage, no matter how mission minded, is exempt from a few missed turns. There's always going to be a few wayward moments. They are a part of every marriage relationship. As Shakespeare put it, "The course of true love never did run smooth." But generally speaking, we can do more than we think to navigate the marriage journey and reach our goal of moving from good to great.

The question is how do we "fix our gaze" and "look straight ahead" as a couple? What can we do as marriage partners to enjoy the comfort and confidence that comes in finding our way together? The answer is found in having a purpose—in having a marital mission that helps us chart our course. Too many couples get lost or bogged down because they forgot why they married to begin with. They had lofty ideals, plans, goals, and dreams as they entered marriage, but amid the demands and hassles of life they eventually lose sight of their "target," end up frittering away their married life, and feel frustrated and aimless as a result.

We've experienced our fair share of matrimonial wandering but in the last few years we've also worked to craft a meaningful purpose statement that helps us keep our marriage on track. In quiet moments of contemplation, accompanied by a cup of coffee, a yellow pad of paper, and a well-worn eraser, we drafted a personal statement that has become our purpose: "Understanding that only God meets all our needs, we will love each other with empathy and try to model a healthy relationship to the young couples we mentor." That's part of our marital mission. And it guides us by keeping our eyes straight ahead, fixed on the path before us.

Drafting a purpose statement for one's marriage isn't every couple's style. That's okay. There are countless ways to keep a marital mission in mind without penning it to paper. We know of a husband who carries a key chain with a small plaque attached that reads: "Love is a decision." It's a meaningful reminder to him that he chose his marriage. And that simple statement helps him cultivate his commitment to his wife. We know a woman who displays on her desk at work a copy of the prayer recited at her wedding. Rereading that prayer takes her back to the "mission" of her marriage. For some couples the simple act of carrying a photo of each other keeps before them the reason they are married.

Some couples, in keeping their eyes on the marriage target, have found it helpful to repeat or revise their wedding vows every few years, or even months. Be it children entering the picture or a major job change, any sudden turn in the road also is reason to fix our eyes as a couple once more on the mission.

Again, marriage mentors can be of great value to another couple wanting to craft a mission statement. You may share your own mission statement and how you arrived at it, for example. You may talk about how it has changed over the years. Or you may simply become a sounding board as you listen to your mentorees try on and shape their own mission statement. However it happens, this issue is often key to moving a couple from good to great.

"Find" More Time to Talk

One of the most common fallacies of time is that you can "find" it. Turn to nearly any business journal or women's magazine and you'll read about ways to "find more time." We talk about time as if it is hidden under the cushion of a chair in our living room or stuck behind a piece of furniture in the basement. Truth is, we'll never find more time. But we can "make" more time by prioritizing what we want. And this can be another powerful way to move a mentoree couple from good to great.

"The reason most goals are not achieved is that we spend our time doing second things first," said Robert J. McKain. And he's exactly right. We may say that our marriage comes first, but that doesn't matter if we devote our time to what's lower on our list. Saying it's a priority and making it a priority are two different things. If your mentorees are merely giving lip service, and not their time, to making their marriage a priority, here is a simple reminder to get them back on track and for making more time in their marriage for talk. It's the secret to reclaiming the conversations they've been missing together.

Drum roll, please. Here it is: Umm ... slow down. No duh!

Right? We did say *simple*. And there's simply no way around the fact that the cure for hurry sickness is to slow down. Lily Tomlin said it best: "For fast-acting relief, try slowing down." If you prefer a more contemplative thinker, here's what Gandhi said: "There is more to life than increasing its speed."

Okay, we all know we should slow down more often, but how? Well, we know one brave mentor couple who does something radical with mentorees they are trying to help in this area. They ask them to surrender their watches and cover every clock in the room when they meet. It's their way of making the point: moving from good to great means keeping your clock from controlling your time together. It forces a couple to ease their foot off the gas pedal of their day and slow down for a meaningful conversation.

In addition, help your mentorees to anticipate their talk time by considering topics they'd like to bring up when they know they will both be relatively relaxed. Have them identify where and when they are likely to have their best talks. Is it over a cup of coffee in the morning? At brunch on a lazy Saturday? In the car when they have a relatively long drive together? These are times they'll want to protect and, again, prioritize.

You get the idea. Oh, and one more practical way to eliminate hurry from your mentorees' conversations? Teach them to drop this sentence from their personal lexicon: "Get to the point." That's a killer for any time-starved conversation.

Our *Love Talk* program (book, men's and women's workbooks, DVD kit, and leader's guide) is dedicated to communication issues and you can learn more about it in appendix 4 of this book. Of course, many other helpful resources are available for helping couples improve their communication, but we've designed *Love Talk* especially with marriage mentors in mind.

Moving from Selfishness to Service

"You're going to vacuum before they get here, right?" Leslie asked in an anxious tone as we were pulling into the garage.

"I've got it under control," I murmured.

We jumped out of the car, each grabbed an armful of groceries, and hurried toward the kitchen. "I'll take care of these groceries so you can get started on the vacuuming," Leslie said. The tension was rising because in less than an hour, two other couples would be at our doorstep expecting a dinner party. "Don't forget to light the candles and turn on the music before they get here," Leslie hollered from the kitchen. I heard what she said but didn't reply as I walked into my study to look through some "urgent" mail.

Only a couple of minutes passed, it seemed to me, when Leslie came into the study and in exasperation asked, "What are you doing?"

"Reading my mail," I responded defensively and with the best look of confusion I could put on my face. She didn't buy it. "Don't worry," I said, "I'll take care of the other stuff." Leslie sighed and left the room. Five minutes later I heard the sound of the vacuum in the living room. *I'm almost done here and then I'll go in and help her,* I said to myself. Ten minutes later the vacuum stopped. I bolted from my chair and walked to the living room. "I thought *I* was going to do this," I said to Leslie. "So did I," she replied.

We've all weaseled our way out of our spouse's "to do" list at one time or another. After all, we've worked hard, we're tired, busy, preoccupied, maxed out, whatever. There's a dozen reasons we use to justify one of the deadliest saboteurs of a healthy marriage: subtle selfishness. It lurks just beneath the surface whenever we are tired and there's a household chore to be done or an errand to be run. That's when we pretend we don't notice the chore or we "forget" about the task, hoping our spouse will take over so we don't have to.

In big and small ways we all squirrel away money, energy, and time for our own advantage, never realizing that we are squandering countless acts of potential kindness and generosity sure to bring us to a deeper level of intimacy and connectedness with our partner.

You see, the problem with subtle self-focus is that it cuts the heart out of marriage. We can rationalize our selfish ways all we want, but we are missing the point of our partnership when we do not pitch in with a generous spirit and help our mate with the task at hand. Subtle selfishness is guaranteed to leave every married couple feeling more like roommates than soul mates. What's worse, it always brings conflict. "For those who are self-seeking," Scripture says (Romans 2:8), "there will be wrath and anger." Spats and tiffs are inevitable whenever we squander kindness and give in to our self-absorption.

Are we saying that there is no place for making one's own needs known? No place for private time or a kind of sanctified self-centeredness in marriage? Nope. We'll even admit that if you live under the same roof long enough your selfish side is bound to emerge and reemerge again and again. Guaranteed. But what we *are* saying is that only when carefully measured and self-focused ways are outweighed by generosity to overflowing can we move from good to great.

This is a continual task where marriage mentors can be of tremendous help. For example, meeting with a mentor couple to review the week for opportunities where selfishness trumped service is guaranteed to be an eye opener. Some mentors will even give their couples an assignment to track this for seven days—not in their partner but in themselves—and then report back. The conversation is always fruitful for couples wanting to move to the next level.

Parenting with Pleasure

Perhaps no other issue is more important in moving a couple from good to great than that of parenting. What weary parents couldn't benefit from meeting with a couple who has already journeyed the road they are on?

Say you are about to have a baby, in just a few months. You want to be sure you do all you can for this new little one but you also want to continue to build a strong marriage. You've read the "what to expect when you're expecting" materials but you've done next to nothing to prepare your marriage for this adjustment. Could a couple who has gone before you be of help? You bet.

Or say you have preschoolers and elementary children busy around your feet. You've never felt more tired. You're still in love but your marital conversations have diminished and your sex life has all but faded as the two of you have moved from being husband and wife to mom and dad. Could a mentor couple who knows the ropes assist you out of your slump and help you breathe some fresh air into your marriage? Of course!

You might be the parents of teenagers. Enough said. A marriage mentor could definitely help!

And, if one or both of you are bringing children from a previous marriage into a second one, there's the humongous issue of blending a family. As marriage expert William Doherty has said, "Stepfamilies are the moral pioneers of contemporary family life, showing us all how to love and persevere in the face of loyalties that multiply and divide, but never fully converge." Could a marriage mentor couple who has successfully blended a family be helpful? Without a doubt.

When it comes to moving couples from good to great, parenting issues simply cannot be avoided. Mom and dad can *still* be husband and wife. Couples who enjoy their relationship to the fullest are living proof of this fact. To be sure, the most important thing a couple may ever do for their children is to work on their marriage. Nothing provides more security and peace in a child's life than knowing that mom and dad are deeply in love. So as you consider mentoring couples from good to great, don't neglect the important issue of parenting.

If ever there was a husband and wife ready to become mom and dad it was Kevin and Judy. With their first baby on the way, their excitement was palpable. They prepared the nursery right down to a neatly ordered stack of diapers, signed up for Lamaze courses, and were reading all the "what to expect" books. Late at night they talked in bed about their future with a baby. What they didn't realize is that they were not only giving birth to a new human but to a new marriage. Ready or not, they were about to be sucked into a huge force that would forever reshape their relationship. Every new mom and dad go through it.

Make no mistake about it, the birth of each child signals a serious and permanent alteration in a marriage. The alteration is, of course, deeply enriching if not miraculous, but for the majority of couples it is also somewhat confusing if not downright challenging. That's where mentors come in.

Studies show that when baby makes three, conflicts increase eightfold; marriage takes a back seat; women feel overburdened, and men feel shoved aside. By the baby's first birthday, most mothers are less happy about their marriage and some are wondering whether their marriage will even make it. Baby-induced marital meltdowns are not uncommon. With the help of researchers such as John Gottman at the University of Washington, here's what we know for sure. In the year after the first baby arrives, 70 percent of wives experience a precipitous plummet in their marital satisfaction. For the husband, the dissatisfaction usually kicks in later, as a reaction to his wife's unhappiness.[1] It has little to do with whether a couple's baby is colicky or a good sleeper, whether she is nursing or bottle-feeding, working or staying at home. It simply has to do with how a new family addition shifts the whole dynamic within a household.

How can something as good as a baby turn a marriage so bad? We could point to a wide range of reasons: lack of sleep, feeling overwhelmed and unappreciated, the awesome responsibility of caring for such a helpless little creature, juggling chores and other economic stress, and lack of time to oneself, among other things. The root reason, however, is no big mystery. In plain language, children take time and attention away from a marriage. They suck all the hours out of the day and fill up every spare cell in your brain. Being a parent is wonderful, only somehow, it's made being a spouse ... different. "Before kids, I was thrilled to hear my husband's voice on the phone," said Judy, a few years into motherhood. "Now after a day of meetings and phone calls and carpools and wet swimsuits, I sometimes wonder who is this guy who seems to want food, an audience, and—he's got to be joking—sex?"

Isn't it romantic? Of course not. But a lack of romance and connection isn't inevitable during this phase of marriage. The fact is, these are the good times and a good mentor couple can help new parents see that. You can teach them, through your own lives, that someday they're going to look back on this period fondly. The experts offer a primary suggestion: expand your sense of "one-ness" to "we-ness" to include your children.

Motherhood brings every new mom a bassinet full of new feelings. She has never felt a love as deep and selfless as the one she feels now. She almost always experiences a profound new sense of meaning in her life and discovers she is willing to make enormous sacrifices for her child. "The experience is so life-altering," says John Gottman, "that if her husband doesn't go through it with her, it is understandable that distance would develop between them." The key to mentoring a good marriage to greatness is to help this new dad to undergo the same intensely wonderful transformation his wife is undergoing. In other words, marital success has everything to do with whether the husband experiences the transformation to parenthood along with his wife. If not, he gets left behind, pining for the old "us" while his wife is embracing a new sense of "we-ness" that includes their child.

A new father often resents how little time his wife has for him (especially in their sex life) now that they have a baby. He resents how tired she always is. He loves his child, but he wants his wife back the way she was. What's a husband to do? Get over his whining and follow her into the new realm she has entered. He has to become a father as well as a husband. He must cultivate feelings of pride, tenderness, and protectiveness for his offspring. In other words, he must see his journey into parenthood as a sign and an opportunity for significant personal growth.

The most wasted of all days is the one without laughter.
E. E. CUMMINGS

If it sounds like we are putting most of the emphasis of your mentoring here on the new dad, it's because we are. The research is clear that this is crucial for the couple who wants to move from good to great. Not that the new mom doesn't factor into the picture. All the responsibility for navigating a good marriage through the unknown channels of parenthood does not rest with the husband alone. A new mother often resents the lack of emotional romance her husband now brings to the marriage. *He's changed,* she may think. *He's more distant.* In actuality, his efforts to embrace this new "we-ness" have probably sidetracked the energy he put into her old expectations of romance. And the more stock she put in romance before the baby was born, the more loss she will feel when her busy husband seems disconnected.

The bottom line? As a new mom and new dad, the couple you may be mentoring each has specific roles to keep a good marriage going. Dad needs to work at entering his wife's new world and mom needs to give her husband space to do so. And they both need to expand their sense of "one-ness" to "we-ness."

The Role of Humor and Laughter

Perhaps the greatest indicator, the most visible fruit, of a couple who is "good" and is well on their way to "great" is laughter. Why? Laughter bonds people. Any good friend will tell you that laugher is the shortest distance between two people — especially in marriage.

But one never knows what's funny to others. In a survey of over 14,000 *Psychology Today* readers who rated thirty jokes, the findings were unequiv-ocal. "Every single joke," it was reported, "had a substantial number of fans who rated it 'very funny,' while another group dismissed it as 'not at all funny.'" Apparently, our funny bones are located in different places. Some laugh uproariously at the slapstick of Larry, Curly, and Moe, while others enjoy the more cerebral humor of Woody Allen.

Wherever you are on this continuum of humor, one thing is certain: Laughter is crucial to mentors wanting to move a marriage from good to great.

Laughter is good medicine, literally. It has important physiological effects. The French philosopher Voltaire wrote, "The art of medicine consists of amusing the patient while nature cures the disease." Modern research indicates that people with a sense of humor have fewer symp-toms of physical illness than those who are less humorous. This idea, of course, isn't new. Since King Solomon's time, people have known about and applied the healing benefits of humor. As Proverbs tells us, "A cheerful heart is good medicine" (17:22).

But humor brings more than physiological benefits to a husband and wife. Humor helps us cope. Consider Janet, who wanted to impress a small group of couples with an elaborate dinner. She cooked all day and enlisted her husband's help to serve the meal. All went well until the main course. As her husband was bringing in the crown roast, the kitchen door hit him from behind and the platter flew across the room. Janet froze, regained her composure, then commanded, "Dear, don't just stand there. Pick up the roast, go in the kitchen, and get the *other* one!"

No doubt about it, humor helps us cope—not just with the trivial but even with the tragic. Psychoanalyst Martin Grotjahn, author of *Beyond Laughter*, notes that "to have a sense of humor is to have an understanding of human suffering." Charlie Chaplin could have said the same thing. Chaplin grew up in the poorest section of London. His mother suffered from serious mental illness and his father died of alcoholism when Charlie was just five. Laughter was Chaplin's tool for coping with life's losses. Eating a boiled leather shoe for dinner in his classic film, *Gold Rush*, is more than a humorous scene. It is an act of human triumph, a monument to the coping power of humor.

One does not need to be a professional comedian, however, to benefit from comedy. All of us can use more laughter in our life. And it's a valuable tool for every marriage mentor who is working with couples who are moving from good to great. When the checkbook doesn't balance, when the kids can't seem to behave, when busy schedules collide, when you can't remember your last date night, not to mention your last vacation—for these times, and dozens of others, humor is invaluable.

Take it from the professionals: Legendary comedian Bob Hope said laughter is an "instant vacation." Jay Leno says, "You can't stay mad at somebody who makes you laugh." And the great Bill Cosby, whose own marriage survived the loss of a son and accusations of infidelity, says, "If you can find humor in anything, you can survive it."

A Final Thought on Moving a Marriage from Good to Great

Greg Clarke, a writer for *Fast Company* magazine, interviewed Jim Collins about companies that move from good to great and he revealed something interesting about how these companies change. In a word: slowly.

Picture an egg. Day after day, it sits there. "No one pays attention to it," writes Clarke. "Then one day, the shell cracks and out jumps a chicken. All of a sudden, the major magazines and newspapers jump on the story: 'Stunning Turnaround at Egg!' From the outside, the story always reads like an overnight sensation—as if the egg had suddenly and radically altered itself into a chicken."

Now picture the egg from the chicken's point of view, urges Clarke. "While the outside world was ignoring this seemingly dormant egg, the chicken within was growing, developing—changing. From the chicken's point of view, the moment of breakthrough, of cracking the egg, was simply one more step in a long chain of steps that had led up to that moment."[2]

Everyone looks for the "miracle moment" when "change happens." But when you ask the good-to-great executives when change happened, they cannot pinpoint a single key event that exemplified their successful transition.

Walgreens is a good example. For more than forty years, Walgreens was no more than an average drugstore chain, tracking the general market. Then in 1975 (out of the blue!) Walgreens began to climb. And climb. And climb. It just kept climbing. Since then, one dollar invested in Walgreens beat one dollar invested in Intel by nearly two times, General Electric by nearly five times, and Coca-Cola by nearly eight times. It beat the general stock market by more than fifteen times.

When Clarke asked a key Walgreens executive to pinpoint when the good-to-great transformation happened, his answer was, "Sometime between 1971 and 1980." Well, that certainly narrows it down! Walgreens's experience is the norm for good-to-great performers — whether it's in business or in marriage.

Lasting change happens slowly. Mentoring couples from good to great is a process. It's not a single switch that's thrown; it doesn't occur overnight. It happens when couples take the time to be intentional about their marriage, exploring the issues we've looked at in this chapter. And this is best done in periodic chunks over increments of time in a marriage mentoring church. And as we can attest from our years of experience of mentoring couples — and mentoring the mentors — it's well worth the effort.

CHAPTER 7

REPAIRING: MENTORING COUPLES IN DISTRESS

You can tell a good, surviving marriage by the expression
in the partners' eyes—like those of sailors who have shared
the battles against foul weather.
  PAM BROWN

Les's father, a pastor, often says that every person will have their own private Gethsemane. It will usually happen in a familiar place. With Jesus it was in the place where he routinely prayed and where Judas knew he could find him. And your Gethsemane will probably include a Judas, someone—maybe even a spouse—who will let you down in ways you never dreamed. In your private Gethsemane you may have close friends who suddenly go to sleep when you need them the most—your Peter, James, and John. You may wonder if their telephones have been disconnected.

Which brings us to the third part of the marriage mentor triad (see the diagram on page 55), and the most serious: couples in crisis and possibly even teetering on the brink of divorce.

Have you suffered a personal Gethsemane? Has your good marriage bumped head-first into something bad? If so, your story and your life may be a powerful marriage mentoring tool for helping couples in distress.

Every congregation has them: couples who are battling addiction, infidelity, infertility, loss, or some other serious difficulty. Often, these are couples on the edge of despair, looking into the abyss. They probably didn't see their crisis coming and, besides, no amount of planning could have prevented the jolt that has struck them. They may have had little or no control over its occurrence—but they *can* control their response to it. With hope and encouragement, with the model of a mentor couple who has gone through it before them, they can walk away from the abyss.

87

Mentoring couples can literally turn couples in crisis around and become instrumental in saving their marriage.

In this chapter, we once more explore the common issues you are likely to see among couples in this category. Specifically, we consider mentoring couples who are battling addiction, infidelity, infertility, or loss. From there we look at some practical programs that may be useful in launching a mentoring ministry to couples in distress.

COMMON WAVES OF CRISIS FACING COUPLES IN DISTRESS

While many cities and villages along the Indian Ocean suffered catastrophic losses from the December 2004 tsunami, the port city of Pondicherry, India, and its 300,000 inhabitants were spared. Just beyond city limits, six hundred people were killed by the devastating tidal wave, but Pondicherry itself withstood the tsunami. Why were they protected?

The answer began 250 years ago when the French who colonized the city initiated the building of a massive stone seawall. Year after year, through 1957, they continued to strengthen the wall, piling huge boulders along its 1.25-mile length. Little did they realize their work prepared the city for a disaster that would occur five decades into the future.

Some marriages are like that port city of Pondicherry. They are well protected from even powerful tsunamis. But most marriages aren't so fortunate. When the unexpected wave bursts upon their relationship they simply do their best to keep their bearings. And that's when the search-and-rescue efforts of marriage mentors save them. In this section we take a look at the most common marital tsunamis and how you might be able to help with any one of them.

> *We are all faced with innumerable opportunities brilliantly disguised as impossible situations.*
>
> BOB RECCORD

But let's make this clear. In nearly all cases, the marriage mentors who are coming alongside these specific couples in crisis should have experienced this crisis before them. In other words, the best mentors for a couple struggling with loss are another couple who has successfully battled loss. Of course, the loss does not have to be exactly the same, but to gain respect and engender hope in the mentorees, they have to see that you know what they are going though.

Let's take a look at each.

Battling Addictions

Greg, a high school basketball coach, blacked out and slipped into unconsciousness during a routine practice with his team. When he came to at the hospital that evening a dark secret began to unravel. Greg was an alcoholic and nobody knew. For eleven years he had been secretly drinking vodka, an odorless libation he had stashed in his garage. Connie, his wife of ten years, sat in shock while Greg laid open his long-standing secret that night at the hospital.

A basketball star in college, Greg had never taken an alcoholic drink in his life until he joined some teammates one evening after a game. "The next morning when I woke up," he later told us, "all I thought about was getting another drink." He did. When he married Connie later that year he was already well into his private addiction and she didn't have a clue.

Now, as Greg's private addiction was exposed, Connie came unglued. She called us from the hospital: "Did you have any idea this was happening?" We were as helpless as she was. It had to be the loneliest night of Connie's life—and her life would never be the same.

Few things divide a couple more than an addiction. Whether it be alcohol, drugs, overeating, or pornography, addiction is as divisive in marriage as an international border. It creates a quiet chasm that grows increasingly wider with each compulsive behavior. If your marriage has been struck by the damage of addiction, we want to make one fundamental point that may help you keep this jolt from ruining your relationship.[1]

Grief and addiction have something in common: denial. The loss of a stable marriage because of addictive involvement generates despair, anger, and loneliness. And because the loss is not as tangible as other losses (the addict is still present), losing a loved one to addiction has the potential of keeping one stuck indefinitely in the early stages of grief—guaranteed to be the undoing of any relationship. Therein is the bind of the "co-addict," or the spouse who wants to mend a broken relationship and winds up unwittingly participating in the same impaired mental processes as the addict.

By definition, the addict replaces normal human relationships with compulsive behavior that is out of control. The spouse who is married to an addict feels the loss, tries to deny it exists, and typically becomes angry. In spite of their despair—or perhaps because of it—they go to extreme lengths to preserve the exterior world of their addicted spouse and their once-happy home.

With your own experience, you probably already know that for some couples this sad cycle goes on for years. Not surprisingly, addictions of all kinds thrive in such relationships. Alcoholism and compulsive overeating may even mingle with sexual addiction in such an environment. The husband justifies his sexual addiction because "she is always drunk." The wife who gains fifty pounds as an expression of her rage is also doing something her husband can't control. Each addiction may involve different behaviors, but they are all crying out for the same remedy: responsibility. The shift of energy from blaming circumstances and other people to taking ownership for feelings and behaviors creates a new environment of trust that is the key to overcoming and recovering from any major problem. The ultimate goal: each spouse taking responsibility, one day at a time.

As a couple who has experienced addiction of some kind yourself, you know how important it is for the addict to get professional help. Your role as marriage mentors is to focus on their marriage in the midst of their recovering. Don't make the mistake of trying to treat the addiction. That's not your role here. You should, however, help the couple secure professional help. As we mentioned in chapter 3, we've included appendix 8, "Spotting Red Flags: When to Refer the Mentoree Couple"—just for this purpose. It outlines the various types of mental health professionals and gives guidance about scheduling an initial meeting.

Surviving Infidelity

Research shows that about 24 percent of men and 14 percent of women have had sex outside their marriages.[2] Though the findings are hotly debated and some argue that these numbers are far too low compared to previous studies, none of that really matters if infidelity has hit your home. All you care about is recovering from the powerful punch to the solar plexus of your relationship.

Marriage mentors working with couples in this sensitive area, who have been there themselves and successfully stayed together, know that a primary question eventually emerges for these couples: *Is it even possible to recover?* The answer, of course, is yes. If two people are willing to slog through the pain and anger of one of the most devastating experiences a husband and wife could ever encounter, they *can* save their marriage.[3] There are countless couples who are living testimonies to the fact that a relationship that has been jolted by unfaithfulness can be restored— perhaps you are one of them!

The number-one goal for both partners, as you know, is to rebuild trust.[4] And you can help your mentorees do just that. In the weeks and months after Rachel's husband Chris had an affair, for example, she found herself doubting him any time he was late coming home or not available when she called him at work. For years she had never questioned him about those things, but with his infidelity fresh in her mind, she had a hard time believing his explanations. To build trust, their mentor couple suggested that Chris let Rachel know when he was away from the office or if he was going to be out later than usual. Though having to check in with his wife made him feel stifled and controlled, he understood. Rachel could see Chris's efforts and desire to be accountable were motivated by wanting to earn her trust. Eventually, she didn't need to check on him as much. After that, Chris's calls became an act of love rather than duty.

In a book like this, we're just not able to explore every issue in depth. But as with the other two legs of the marriage mentoring triad, we have developed a practical mentoring program for mentors to use with couples in distress. It's called *I Love You More*. And again, you can learn more about this program (book, men's and women's workbooks, DVD kit, and leader's guide) in appendix 6.

We should mention another valuable resource in setting up a mentoring ministry to couples in distress called "Retrouvaille"—it rhymes with apple pie and is French for "rediscovery." And that's just what this program provides for a couple who has disconnected from each other—a chance to rediscover oneself, one's spouse, and their loving relationship. Thousands of couples headed for divorce have successfully saved their marriages through the help of Retrouvaille.

Designed especially for couples experiencing affairs, alcoholism, gambling addictions, violence, and so on, the program links trained, volunteer mentor couples who have "been to the brink" and are now back in a healthy marriage with couples who are dangerously close to the brink themselves.

Is Retrouvaille successful? It has an 85 percent success rate for couples where both partners work at it together. With an emphasis on communication, forgiveness, healing, and restoration of trust, the program begins with a weekend away and includes twelve follow-up meetings over three months. These are not spiritual retreats, sensitivity groups, seminars, or social gatherings—there are no counselors involved and you don't have to say anything in front of anyone else. Couples discuss the topics and practice skills in privacy. The financial cost? It's run on a blank-envelope-donation system.

If you are interested in this tremendous resource for couples in distress, you can learn more at www.retrouvaille.org. Browse their website to read some of the success stories, find a weekend meeting near you, and more. Any marriage mentor working on the reparative side of the mentoring triad needs to become aware of Retrouvaille.

As mentors to couples with such issues, you will see just how incredible it is when what once appeared to be an irreparable wound is transformed into a catalyst for growth in marriage. You will witness, time and again, that with God's help and healing, even the most serious betrayal can be overcome when a person makes right what has gone wrong.

Coping with Infertility

Half of all Americans who try to get pregnant have trouble doing so and one in six couples in the United States are jolted by infertility—the inability to conceive a child after trying for a year or more.[5] These couples

---

Advice to a Couple in the Crisis of Infidelity

To the spouse who had the affair:

First and foremost, sever all contact with the third party immediately. Clear boundaries need to be established if you want to rebuild the trust you have broken with your partner.

You must be willing to answer any questions from your spouse. This is not because your partner needs to know all the details of what went on, but they need to know they have your *willingness* to give them the details. It shows respect, honor, and equality and that you can be trusted in the future.

To the spouse who has remained faithful:

You should only ask questions if you really want the truth. Some things may be better left alone if you are able to do so. You also must steer clear of the temptation to use any information you receive as a way to "beat up" your partner for other problems down the road.

Remember, it may take years to absorb the emotional impact of what has happened. Adultery is not something you can get over quickly. It's important to give yourself plenty of time to recover.

not only make a financial sacrifice and commit a substantial amount of time to undergo intrusive medical tests and treatments, but their marriage is often turned inside out. What was once a passionate exchange becomes a scheduled exercise fraught with anxiety about failing again to conceive. Partners feel angry with their bodies and struggle with the thorny question of whether to keep their medical trials secret from family and friends. Hovering above all of these decisions is the disappointing possibility that there is no guarantee they will ever conceive a child.[6]

If you are mentoring a couple in this area, you have likely struggled with the emotional assault of infertility yourself. You know the pangs of sadness. Most likely, every area of your life has been impacted—from career decisions, to sexuality, to relationships with friends and extended family members. But since you are at a place of mentoring others, you have some sense of contentment and closure. Obviously, you cannot mentor another couple about infertility if you haven't.

Most couples struggling with infertility travel through some fairly predictable passages. First is preoccupation with why this is happening. *What have we done wrong? Why are we so defective? Why are we denied something the rest of the world takes for granted?* Next comes mourning the loss of bearing children and undergoing an intense soul-searching of what parenting means as individuals, as a couple, and as members of an extended family and society. Finally, over time, these couples enter a decision-making phase about pursuing adoption or adjusting to childlessness and seeking fulfillment in other areas of life. This is also the stage in which they must realign the disjointedness their marriage has endured as a result of their journey.

How does a couple best do this? By healing the sometimes private wounds each partner has suffered in the process. Whether they are just coming to terms with being childless as a couple or they have been at this place for many years, it is imperative for the life of their relationship that they attend to any lingering loose ends—especially ones either partner may not know about.

Helping each partner heal their private wounds suffered through their own journey of infertility does not guarantee a "happy" ending of the struggle, but it does significantly increase the odds of keeping infertility from tearing at the fabric of their marriage.

Dealing with Loss

Few things jolt our personhood, our marriage, our very core, more severely than loss. Whether it be loss of a job through injury or circumstances, the loss of money due to a soured investment, the loss of a sibling due to emotional turmoil, the loss of a friend or loved one due to tragedy or natural causes, the loss of a child in a custody dispute from a previous marriage — loss creates one of the loneliest experiences on earth, even in the middle of a good marriage.

You probably know the stages: numbing disbelief, yearning and searching, disorganization and despair. Collectively we call it grief. Though highly individual, it is a process, not an event, that always takes time. It can't be rushed or compressed. The grief process, though painful in many ways, has its own internal logic; if allowed to proceed, it almost always resolves successfully. In the end, grief takes us to a new place and helps us reorganize our life and move forward.

As grief does its work, however, it can wreak havoc on a marriage. For this reason one of the most important things marriage mentors can do for a couple trying to cope with loss is to help them keep clear the channels of communication. Without an open and honest dialogue, a husband and wife will unknowingly build barriers around their hearts. They will journey separate paths and lose touch with one another. They will miss out on one of the great gifts of being married.

Keeping communication channels open requires vulnerability. It demands the exposure of real feelings. If, as a mentor couple, you are not up to the challenge of being in the midst of this raw emotion, if you are not comfortable with tears rolling down another couple's cheeks, you may want to mentor in a different area.

By the way, keeping communication honest and open while grieving is not always safe, but it is good. C. S. Lewis's children's classic *The Lion, the Witch, and the Wardrobe* includes a scene in which one of the main characters, a young girl named Lucy, first encounters Aslan, the great lion. Lucy sees Aslan and exclaims with trepidation to one of the talking animals, "Is he safe?" The animal responds, "Safe?" Who said anything about being safe? 'Course he isn't safe. But he's good."

Grieving a loss isn't always safe, either. It's not predictable. You can't control how another couple will respond to frightening feelings. But the process is good. And as a mentor couple, it many be one of the greatest gifts you can ever give.

Can You Predict a Marriage Crisis?

A couple who is characterized by several of these identifiers is more likely to experience a marital crisis—though no marriage is immune to serious problems *and* though none of these situations is certain to lead to difficulties:

- The couple meets or marries shortly after a significant loss (for example, the death of a parent).
- The wish to distance from one's family of origin is a factor in the marriage.
- The family backgrounds of each spouse are significantly different (religion, education, social class, ethnicity, and so on).
- The couple resides either extremely close to or at a great distance from either family of origin.
- The couple is overly dependent on either extended family.
- The couple marries before age twenty.
- The couple marries after an acquaintanceship of less than six months.
- The couple marries after more than three years of engagement.
- The wedding occurs without family or friends present.
- The wife becomes pregnant before or within the first year of marriage.
- Either spouse has a poor relationship with his or her siblings or parents.
- Either spouse considers his or her childhood or adolescence an unhappy time.
- Marital patterns in either family were unstable.

A FINAL THOUGHT ON MENTORING COUPLES IN DISTRESS

We know a couple, Bill and Lydia, who suffered a major loss at a critical time of their lives. Bill had worked for many years as an executive in a national corporation. Taking early retirement, he turned over his big chunk of severance pay to a friend who had a financial deal that "could not miss." But it did. Bill and Lydia, both in their mid-sixties, found themselves scrambling to live on an inadequate income after their investments had drained dry. It was a huge jolt. Lesser people have been known to destroy themselves in the face of such a problem. Not Bill and Lydia. They moved from a big fashionable house to a small bungalow. They traded in their big car for a small economy model. Instead of sitting back and enjoying his retirement, Bill became a meter reader for a public utility company.

Bill and Lydia had every reason to be bitter. Instead, they determined to adjust their attitude to a serious problem that was beyond their control. How did they do it? Through a whole lot of prayer, a decision to overcome it, and the help of a mentor couple who had experienced similar circumstances. If you were to meet Bill and Lydia, you would have no idea they'd ever suffered such a setback. Though it took time to grieve their loss, they are happy in spite of their circumstances.

> *Circumstances may appear to wreck our lives and God's plans, but God is not helpless among the ruins. Our broken lives are not lost or useless. God's love is still working. He comes in and takes the calamity and uses it victoriously, working out his wonderful plan of love.*
> ERIC LIDDELL

Whatever your private Gethsemane may entail, you can use it to minister in a profound way to other couples who have experienced similar circumstances. You picked yourselves up, you bounced back—together. You have a wonderful gift that can benefit others. And remember this: there is nothing more fulfilling than playing a role in helping a married couple battle something bad and win.

PART THREE

The ESSENTIAL SKILLS for MARRIAGE MENTORING

When love and skill work together,
expect a masterpiece.

JOHN RUSKIN

In this final section we roll up our sleeves and show you in very practical terms the skills that every effective marriage mentor must master. These are the fundamentals that apply to mentoring at all levels, whether you are mentoring engaged and newlywed couples, couples in distress, or couples wanting to move from good to great. This section is valuable not only to couples who are doing the mentoring, but also to pastors and other church leaders who oversee the marriage mentoring program in a local church.

How do we know these qualities are essential? Because we've conducted empirical research on training marriage mentors. We know the value of this training. It bolsters confidence and sharpens the mentor's effectiveness.[7]

A forthcoming DVD kit featuring many marriage mentors and mentorees accompanies this part of the book and is an ideal way for learning each of these skills. In addition, after viewing this DVD series (six sessions) you will be eligible to take the online review questionnaire and receive a personalized certificate of completion. You can learn more about this training process at www.RealRelationships.com.

CHAPTER 8

BUILDING RAPPORT

There is no substitute for the comfort supplied
by the utterly taken-for-granted relationship.
IRIS MURDOCH

Nothing reaches so deeply into the human personality or tugs so tightly as relationship. Why? For one reason, it is only in the context of connection with others that our deepest needs can be met. Whether we like it or not, each of us has an unshakable dependence on others. It's what philosopher John Donne was getting at when he said so succinctly, "No man is an island." We need camaraderie, affection, solidarity, commonality, love. These are not options in life, or sentimental trimmings; they are part of our species' survival kit. We need relationships.

Human relationships always help us to carry on because they always presuppose a future.
ALBERT CAMUS

Social scientists call our longing for belonging by such terms as assimilation, affiliation, or social webbing. Others call it fellowship, connecting, or relating. Whatever it's called, everyone agrees that we're born with an insatiable inner need for meaningful interaction with others. And make no mistake, no one is too big, strong, talented, or tough to go without relationships. The best things in life happen as a result of our relationships. We laugh in relationships. We commiserate in relationships. And we learn in relationships.

That's why the first order of business in becoming effective as a marriage mentor is to master the fine art of building rapport. In chapter 2, we touched on this ability when we discussed personal warmth. A mentor who possesses warmth brings a sense of relaxation and comfort to the relationship. That's what rapport is all about.

Rapport in a mentoring relationship is built and sustained on conveying personal warmth. Rapport is a process of establishing a relationship of trust, harmony, and affinity. It is a relationship typified by cooperation, agreement, and alignment. Having rapport with another results in feelings of comfort, satisfaction, and a sense of shared understanding.

Establishing rapport suggests several messages to the couples you mentor: "We are like you"; "We are in sync with you"; and "You can trust us." Rapport tends to minimize differences and harmonize experiences and values. It accentuates similarities and downplays differences so that understanding and a sense of connection are increased and maintained. In David Stoddard's book *The Heart of Mentoring*, he observes, "Unless I can come to know what is real about you — something of your life story, what you care about and stand for, what you feel as well as what you know — you do not actually exist for me beyond your name, job title and appearance.... When we get inspired and motivated, it is by real people, the ones with a good head on their shoulders, of course, but always with a heart. No one expects a [mentor] to be perfect — only genuine and honest.... [Such people possess] the courage to find themselves, to tell the truth about who they are, the mistakes they have made, the dreams they hold and what they're most concerned about, and excited about, in ... growing their life. This is the bedrock for open dialogue and trust."[1]

So how do you go about building rapport? It's easier than you might think. Our answer has to do with three simple tasks: (1) identifying with the couple, (2) establishing credibility with them, and (3) monitoring your interest in them. Let's take a closer look at each of these steps.

IDENTIFY WITH YOUR MENTOREES

For most mentors, this comes rather naturally. After all, you are mentoring a particular couple precisely because you have been where they are now. You have things in common. Whether you are mentoring a newlywed couple, a couple about to have a baby, a couple struggling with an addiction or debt or any other predicament, you are with them because of your similarities. For this reason, identifying with your mentoree couple, normally, should not require much work. If it does, then this particular mentoring relationship probably should be reconsidered.

Still, the idea of identifying at a deep level is worthy of exploration. How can you maximize your natural inclination to identify with a particular couple? Body posture is a fundamental starting point. When we identify with someone, our body posture relaxes as do our breathing and voice patterns. The tone and tempo of our speech matches the person we are identifying with. When they get excited, we get excited. When they're contemplative, so are we.

Language is another important point of identifying. When your mentorees use particular words that they seem to highly value (experts call these "criteria" words), you want to pay attention and use them as well. For example, you may find that they keep talking about their "challenge." They may say something like, "Everything is going pretty well for us but we keep bumping into this one challenge," or "Our biggest challenge is dealing with our in-laws." Or maybe you pick up on them using the word *growth* frequently. The idea is not to parrot back to the couple whatever they say. The point is to be cognizant of any words that appear to carry special emphasis or meaning for them.

Of course, all this identifying goes both ways. Mentorees identify with you. And that leads to the next key ingredient to building rapport: credibility.

ESTABLISH CREDIBILITY WITH YOUR MENTOREES

Credibility is the quality of being believable or trustworthy. It is defined by *Webster's Collegiate Dictionary* as "the quality or power of inspiring belief." When applied to marriage mentoring, credibility centers on three factors for the mentorees:

Opportunity—*Are our marriage mentors in a position to know what we need?* In other words, do you have a personal history that will allow you to understand the mentorees in a way that other couples may not?

Ability—*Do our marriage mentors have the skill and competence to mentor us?* Mentorees want to be assured that you not only have a history that will give you insight into their situation, but that you also have the know-how to make a difference.

Dependability—*Are our marriage mentors responsible and trustworthy?* Mentorees want to know that you are invested in them, that you will be there for them in this mentoring process and that you are not simply going through the motions.

When your mentorees can positively answer the questions related to these three factors, you can be assured that you have established a deep level of credibility. This means that you have their trust—a precious possession indeed.

MONITOR YOUR INTEREST LEVEL IN YOUR MENTOREES

Once you identify with your mentorees and have established credibility, you have one final objective in solidifying a strong sense of rapport. You need to keep an eye on your ability to stay tuned in. Why? Because rapport fades the moment your mentorees think you might be losing interest. If you come off as more concerned about sports scores or what time it is or anything else, they will notice your distraction. A little distraction from time to time, of course, is only human. But if you are truly losing interest in your mentoree couple, it's time to reconsider your relationship because your heart's not in it.

As Proverbs 16:23 says, "A wise man's heart guides his mouth, and his lips promote instruction." You can talk about mentoring and instruction all you want, but if your heart's not in it, the relationship will surely fall flat. Effective mentoring hinges on being genuinely interested and invested in your mentorees because your level of interest is essential to building rapport.

There you have it. When it comes to building rapport, three simple tasks are involved: (1) identifying with the couple, (2) establishing credibility with them, and (3) monitoring your interest in them. This is not to deny the reality that some aspects of rapport we can't easily produce. As in any relationship, we can establish good relational habits, but some aspects of the attraction remain a mystery left to the Holy Spirit.

Another important aspect of your relationship with your mentorees, certain to enrich your rapport with them, is the ability to put yourselves in their shoes. Let's look in the next chapter at what this means.

REAL-LIFE EXAMPLE OF *Building Rapport*

Steve and Sandy, married eleven years, were a little apprehensive about meeting their first mentoree couple. They'd volunteered to mentor newly-wed couples and were primarily nervous about "clicking." That was their word for building rapport.

"I just hope they like and respect us," Sandy confided. "I mean, if they don't like us there's not much we can do for them as mentors." And she's right. That's why they worked hard to cultivate a warm sense of rapport.

It began by identifying with the newlywed couple assigned to them. Soon into their first conversation, they realized that though they were from different parts of the country, they had both moved to their present town from large cities. They talked about the adjustments that these moves had involved and then learned that each of them had dated the same amount of time — three years — before getting married. After talking a little bit about their wedding ceremonies, they also discovered that each couple had honeymooned on the California coast. Other similarities were discovered: both couples loved dogs, backpacking, and movies. When their mentorees talked about being "soul mates," Steve and Sandy were quick to pick up on that phrase and explored it with them. "Being 'soul mates' is important to us, too. What does it mean to you guys?"

With a sense of common identity firmly in place, Steve and Sandy also focused on credibility. Their mentorees respected the fact that Steve and Sandy had been married more than a decade and were still very much in love. "You can tell how much they enjoy being together," the mentorees said. "We just like watching them, how they interact and everything." But do their mentorees trust their abilities? When it came to exploring finances and setting up a budget, they soon saw that they were in good hands. For example, Steve, the owner of a small business, talked about how his business skills had helped him and Sandy when it came to their finances as a couple.

A sense of dependability emerged over time as Steve and Sandy met unfailingly with their mentorees and told them flat out: "We are here for you." And they were. They were consistent in their commitment and interest level in their mentorees, solidifying a strong sense of rapport.

CHAPTER 9

WALKING IN ANOTHER COUPLE'S SHOES

You give but little when you give of your possessions.
It is when you give of yourself that you truly give.
KAHLIL GIBRAN

Angela teetered as she walked across a medical conference room, thighs chafing, sweat glands sweating. She tried to squeeze into a regular-size chair, but her hips snagged on the arms. She moved to an extra-wide armless chair, but then she couldn't cross her legs.

A dietitian helped her climb aboard a stationary bicycle that had been fitted with an oversize seat. But when Angela tried to pedal, rolls of abdominal tissue pressed against her thighs, impeding movement.

"Every move I made was an effort," Angela later admitted. By then, however, she was slimmed down to her actual weight: 110 pounds.

Angela had been zipped into a bulky, beige "empathy suit" designed to help medical personnel better understand the plight of their obese patients. The suit weighs only thirty pounds, but it feels heavier and effectively simulates for people like Angela what the workaday world of the obese is like.[1]

Does it work? You bet. Angela saw firsthand that even a simple movement such as walking may be challenging for the obese. Having worn the suit "makes me feel more respectful, more aware of their feelings," she says.

That's the power of putting oneself in the skin of another—literally. Consider almost any profession. For example, you can improve a second-grade teacher's effectiveness by having her walk through her classroom on her knees. As she sees that space from a second grader's perspective, she will naturally be better equipped to teach them. Or how about serving fast food? The major chains spend bundles of money sending "fake customers" into their stores to get their reaction. Advertising firms on Madison Avenue make their living by putting themselves in the consumer's shoes. Growing churches are growing because they study the experience of a first-time visitor and the pastor imagines what it is like to sit in the pew. Disneyland's "cast members" know that guests will average sixty contact opportunities in a single day at their theme park and they want to make each of them a magic moment; so they continually work at empathizing with families.[2] Of course, a counselor wouldn't last a day without practicing empathy. And the same holds true for marriage mentors.

In fact, it is difficult to exaggerate the importance of empathy to marriage mentoring. You can empathize without being a mentor, but you cannot mentor without empathy. So in this chapter we will explore this invaluable marriage mentoring skill. And we begin by attempting to underscore its consequence before rolling up our sleeves to show you how you can do it better.

HOW WELL YOU EMPATHIZE DETERMINES HOW WELL YOU MENTOR

The point is that empathy, the ability to accurately see the world through another's eyes, is at the heart of true understanding. We believe that empathy is so vital to marriage mentoring that we often say your success in this endeavor will rise or fall based on how well you empathize with your mentorees.

You won't find the word *empathy* in the New Testament, but the idea is captured strongly in the biblical word *compassion*. It's a natural response of Jesus to the suffering around him (see, for example, Matthew 9:36; 14:14; 20:34), a theme in parables such as the good Samaritan (Luke 10:33) and the prodigal son (Luke 15:20), and an ongoing command in the epistles (see Ephesians 4:32; Colossians 3:12; 1 John 3:17–18). The essence of New Testament compassion is recognition of and concern for another's need *and* appropriate action to meet that need.

Without empathy, healthy relationships are impossible. Consider your contentment when another person senses what you are feeling without you having to say so. This is the essence of empathy. While we can have interesting conversations and smooth social exchanges without it, we will never enter the inner chambers of a person's heart without empathy. It is the key to unlocking a person's spirit at the most intimate and vulnerable levels.

If asking a string of quality questions is the equivalent of a BA in relationships, empathy will earn you your PhD in the social arts. Empathy is evidence of relational brilliance.

Yale psychologist Peter Salovey and the University of New Hampshire's John Mayer coined the term *emotional intelligence* in 1990 to describe qualities that bring human interactions to their peak of performance. Harvard psychologist and *New York Times* science writer Daniel Goleman brought the phrase into the national conversation with his groundbreaking book on the subject. He calls empathy our "social radar" and believes it operates at different levels. At the very least, empathy enables us to read another's emotions; at a higher level, it entails sensing a person's unspoken concerns, and at the highest levels, empathy is understanding the concerns that lie behind the person's feelings.

The key to identifying and understanding another person's emotional terrain, experts agree, is an intimate familiarity with one's own. Goleman cites the research of Robert Levenson at the University of California at Berkeley as a prime example.[3] Levenson brings married couples into his physiology lab for two discussions: a neutral talk about their day and a second fifteen-minute emotionally charged discussion concerning a disagreement. Levenson records the husband's and wife's heart rates, muscle tension, changes in facial expressions, and so on. After the disagreement, one partner leaves. A replay of the talk is then narrated by the other partner, noting feelings on their end that were not expressed. Then the roles are reversed and that partner leaves, allowing the other person to narrate the same scene from his or her partner's perspective.

The great gift of human beings is that we have the power of empathy.
MERYL STREEP

This is where something extraordinary is found. Partners adept at empathizing were seen to mimic their partner's body while they empathize. If the heart rate of the partner in the videotape goes up, so does the heart rate of the partner who is empathizing; if the heart rate slows down, so does that of the empathic spouse. It is a phenomenon called "entrainment" and it demands we put aside our own emotional agendas for the time being to clearly receive the other person's signals. As Goleman says, "When we are caught up in our own strong emotions, we are off on a different physiological vector, impervious to the more subtle cues that allow rapport."[4]

Putting aside our own emotional agenda for empathy's sake brings us to a question we often pose to mentors: What races through your head when you walk into a room to meet your mentorees? If you are not quietly asking yourself "How is this couple doing?" you will never provide the psychological and spiritual space for empathy to do its work. But when you do, you will begin to enjoy a profound relational connection with your mentorees.

How to Empathize with Your Mentorees

Let's make an important clarification: empathy is deeper and stronger than sympathy. Sympathy is standing on the shore and throwing out a lifeline to someone struggling in the water. Every decent human being — marriage mentor or not — sympathizes. It flows with the adrenaline. We barely have to think about it. Sympathy requires no training or skill. It's not terribly deliberate. We sympathize with a couple when we automatically feel what they feel.

Empathy, on the other hand, is more daring, more deliberate. Empathy is jumping into the water and risking one's own safety to help a person who is struggling. And the risk is real. Why? Because empathy will change you. Once you empathize with someone, once you accurately understand what life must be like to be lived in their skin, you'll never see that person the same way again. You'll have more patience with them, more grace and compassion for them.

The difference between sympathy and empathy? Empathy involves both your head and your heart. It requires you to analyze as well as sympathize. It requires you to be both objective and subjective. That's the challenge of empathy. So how can you do it better?

First, you need to consciously and deliberately put yourself in your mentorees' shoes. Consider their age, how long they've been married, the homes they grew up in, their level of education. What are their aspirations and dreams? What pressures weigh on them? How might their jobs or financial situation impact their relationship? And how are children influencing their marriage? The goal for this first step is to get your head and heart into their world and see it from their perspective.

Next, you need to ask an important question: How would I feel if I were in their shoes? In other words, what emotions would you carry if you were living in their place? Would you be content? Why or why not? What would bring you the greatest relief? What would trouble you most? What would bring you the most happiness if you were in their shoes? The goal here is to imagine how you would feel if you were them.

Third, you need to step out of your emotions and get objective. Realize that you are not them. And that how you would feel if you were them is only a projection. They may have a completely different emotional experience about some aspect of their life than you would have. How do you do this? By asking them to help you. You might say, "I know how I would feel if I were in your shoes, but I'm not you. How are you feeling about this?" This requires you to remove your own feelings about the situation and not judge their emotional experience.

Finally, ask God to help you accurately understand your mentorees as you work to empathize with them. Pray that God would help you balance your head and your heart in this process. Empathy is one of the most Christlike actions we ever perform and if we are to do it well it will be because we allow the Holy Spirit to do it through us.

Perhaps a word of caution is in order. A respected colleague has remarked that the most effective mentor couples hang on to their wisdom and act their age. Yet they do not lose their connection with the following generations. What do we mean by this? Have you ever seen a fifty- or sixty-year-old person who tries to dress and talk like a twenty-year-old? How patently absurd. Obviously this person hasn't matured and doesn't act their age. Most twenty-somethings look at that person and see a fraud or fool. Contrast that with an eighty-year-old couple we once met who never lost their zeal for living and their passion for caring. After moving from their longtime home in California to the eastern slope of Colorado, they lived temporarily in a small apartment complex while their home was being built. As part of their daily routine they began having meals at a diner a few blocks away. Because of their regularity they developed a first-name acquaintance with many of the twenty-something wait staff. They asked questions, laughed with them, and showed

> *Two parts of empathy: Skill (tip of iceberg) and Attitude (mass of the iceberg).*
>
> ANONYMOUS

genuine interest. Eventually this couple decided to invite some of these younger people over for meals and "roundtable" discussions about life, relationships, and God. The small groups turned into big groups as the young people told their friends. Several came to faith in Christ and many made important life decisions. It all began with an ability to show empathy.

While these first two marriage mentoring skills of building rapport and walking in another couple's shoes focus on your relationship with your mentorees, the next skill, discussed in chapter 10, focuses more on you as a couple and your ability to work as a team.

REAL-LIFE EXAMPLE OF *Walking in Another Couple's Shoes*

Aimee and Thomas, married seventeen years, are mentoring an engaged couple who has just set their wedding date and agreed to abide by the church's premarital policy for the seven months in the interim. The couple is attending a seven-session premarriage class, two one-on-one meetings with a pastor, and meeting monthly with Aimee and Thomas as their mentor couple.

In their first meeting with Aimee and Thomas the engaged couple revealed that they had been living together for the past three months, which is what helped them decide to get married. "We had been dating for nearly five months when we decided to save some money by living in the same apartment," they told their mentors.

Internally, Aimee and Thomas bristled. They knew this was against their church's premarriage policy. And so did the mentorees. "To get married at this church we knew we needed to not live together but we haven't gotten around to making that happen."

"My first impulse," said Thomas, "was to whip out the policy agreement they signed and show them how they were not being truthful. My next impulse was to call the pastor and tell him that this couple shouldn't be in our program." But Thomas didn't do that. Thanks to Aimee, who patiently asked the couple a few questions about their financial situation, Thomas took a few moments to garner some perspective and, along with Aimee, put himself in this couple's shoes.

"We certainly didn't live together before we got married, so this took some real effort," he confided. "But I worked at it. I asked myself how I would feel if I were them — a couple new to the church who had never had any biblical instruction on cohabitation. I asked myself how I would feel about it if it made good financial sense. In other words, I did my best to imagine how things would look to me if I were them."

Aimee did the same thing. What difference did it make? Plenty. They approached the situation with more compassion and sensitivity. "This policy may seem kind of strange to you two, I imagine," Thomas said to them.

"You got that right," the young man agreed. "What difference does it make if we are going to be living together seven months from now?"

This genuine question opened the door for Thomas and Aimee to talk, in a very gracious tone, about why the church had this policy against cohabitation. Because they empathized with the engaged couple, they created a safe place for genuine understanding and teaching to occur. They explained that it was not only a biblical mandate but that it made good sense for the future of their relationship (secular research backs it up). In the end, the couple agreed to the policy and expressed deep appreciation for the way Aimee and Thomas handled it.

CHAPTER 10

WORKING AS A TEAM

You can do what I cannot do.
I can do what you cannot do.
Together we can do great things.
MOTHER TERESA

In his book *None of These Diseases*, S. I. McMillen tells a story of a young woman who wanted to go to college, but her heart sank when she read the question on the application blank that asked, "Are you a leader?"

Being both honest and conscientious, she wrote, "No," and returned the application, expecting the worst. To her surprise, she received this letter from the college: "Dear Applicant: A study of the application forms reveals that this year our college will have 1,452 new leaders. We are accepting you because we feel it is imperative that they have at least one follower."

So how would you answer that question? Are you a leader? How about your spouse? The truth is, when it comes to marriage mentoring, it takes two leaders working in tandem. And that's not always an easy task. It requires some skill. Why? Because, one moment one of you may be taking the lead while the very next the other person will step in to focus direction. In other words, marriage mentoring requires passing the leadership baton back and forth, or more accurately, sharing it. You have to work as a team.

A biblical example of teamwork can be seen in the New Testament story of the apostle Paul's associates, Aquila and his wife Priscilla. Paul met them in the Greek city of Corinth after they had fled the city of Rome because Claudius had ordered the deportation of all Jews. The couple opened up their home to Paul and worked with him as a team in his efforts to evangelize in the synagogues of their adopted city. Together this married couple owned a tentmaking and leatherworking firm, with branches of the business at Rome, Corinth, and Ephesus. Since Paul also had skill as a tentmaker you can see why he had an obvious rapport with them.

This couple became so valuable as Paul's team members that when it came time for him to sail to Syria, he took them along and then left them off in Ephesus. Later you'll recall that Paul wrote to the Christians in Rome, the city where the couple had originally lived, and said, "Greet Priscilla and Aquila, my fellow workers in Christ Jesus. They risked their lives for me. Not only I but all the churches of the Gentiles are grateful to them. Greet also the church that meets at their house" (Romans 16:3–5). Paul adds a similar greeting at the end of his first letter to the Corinthians: "Aquila and Priscilla greet you warmly in the Lord, and so does the church that meets at their house" (1 Corinthians 16:19). The same thing happens in 2 Timothy 4:19: "Greet Priscilla and Aquila." Working together as a team creates bonds. We wonder if the fact that the church met in their home provided an occasion for them to mentor other married couples. Perhaps you know couples like Aquila and Priscilla in your church; perhaps you are such a couple yourself.

Chances are that you're already pretty good at working as a team but let us highlight three points that may help you ensure your teamwork as a marriage mentor couple: (1) understand your unique strengths, (2) empower each other's voice, and (3) embrace your differences.

UNDERSTAND EACH OTHER'S STRENGTHS

NFL champion coach Vince Lombardi observed, "The achievements of an organization are the result of the combined effort of each individual." The same is true for marriage mentoring. As a good team, the two of you need to know and understand what each of you is most uniquely gifted at as a mentor. For example, one of you might be better at setting up a structure for your meetings while the other is better at helping to build rapport. Maybe one of you is particularly good at exploring financial matters while the other is gifted at resolving conflicts.

As marriage mentors ourselves, I (Les) often found that I look to Leslie to bring closure to a conversation with our mentorees. She seems to have a knack for bringing everything together after a lengthy conversation and clarifying the next step. I (Leslie), on the other hand, know that Les feels more comfortable than I do in initiating a topic of conversation that might heighten anxiety.

You get the idea. The point is to talk about your comfort zones. Avoid making assumptions about each other and get your strengths out on the table. Of course, some of this will be revealed as you gain more mentoring experience, but chances are that you are aware of some of these strengths right now.

EMPOWER EACH OTHER'S VOICE

Consider a tuning fork. It delivers a true pitch by two tines vibrating together. Muffle either side, even a little, and the note disappears. Neither individual tine produces the sweet, pure note. Only when both tines vibrate is the correct pitch heard.

This beautifully illustrates the point of working together as a couple-team. If one of your voices is muffled in the mentoring process, true marriage mentoring disappears. What you are doing as a couple is, in great part, unquantifiable. Your very presence and interaction together in front of your mentorees is your true value to them. Sure, what you say to them and anything you might teach them is important, but it's your modeling as a married couple, it's your relationship that speaks the loudest.

How do you empower each other's voice as you mentor? One of the best ways is to echo each other's points. That is, to underscore what your spouse is saying. When he says he can relate to the mentoree husband who is feeling intimidated by his father-in-law, for example, you might say, "It's true." You might turn to your husband and say, "I remember you feeling the same way a few years ago." This not only reinforces your partner's point, but it keeps both of you fully engaged in the conversation. It keeps both of your voices strong.

Another way to do this is to ask each other questions. Many times mentors think questioning is only to be directed to mentorees. Not so. It can be very helpful to turn to your partner in the course of your mentor meeting and genuinely ask, "What do you think about what she's saying?" or "I bet you might have some thoughts on this issue." It's an invitation that shows your mentorees that you value each other's input. In other words, you can tee the proverbial ball up for each other so that it can more easily be moved down the fairway. That's teamwork.

EMBRACE YOUR DIFFERENCES

Working together as a marriage mentor team does not mean automatic agreement. Even as you empower each other's voice, you can certainly disagree. You have to be true to your own thinking and feeling. If your partner holds a different position than you do on parenting teenagers, for example, you need not stifle your opinion. In fact, your mentorees can learn much from watching the two of you successfully navigate your differences.

"Seeing Peggy accept the fact that Randall didn't agree with the way she parents in some areas was inspiring to us," said one mentoree couple. "It kind of freed us from having to be exactly the same on each issue; we loosened up a little because of it." The point? Peggy and Randall weren't directly teaching them about managing differences, it simply emerged and it was a powerful message: We may have differences but we are still a team.

Ask not what your teammates can do for you. Ask what you can do for your teammates.

EARVIN "MAGIC" JOHNSON

Now, if you have a difference that is raw and unresolved in your marriage, your session with your mentorees is not the place to explore it. The differences we are talking about exposing here have to do with issues that will not surprise or threaten your partner. We're talking about embracing the differences you have learned to manage and live with.

As we said at the outset, you're probably already pretty good at working as a team. You wouldn't volunteer to serve as a marriage mentor couple if that weren't the case. Still, it never hurts to remember your unique strengths, empower each other's voice, and embrace each other's differences.

So far we've looked at three essential skills: building rapport, walking in another's shoes, and working as a team. In the next chapter we'll focus your marriage mentoring teamwork on your purpose — agreeing on outcomes.

Working as a Team

Jeff and Melinda, married thirty-eight years, work wonderfully as a team. It hasn't always been that way, however. About eighteen years ago, Melinda found out that Jeff had been having an affair with a female colleague at work. Needless to say, she was devastated and their marriage was definitely up for grabs. But through some effective counseling, a lot of repentance and forgiveness, the earning back of trust on Jeff's part, and a drastic change in lifestyle, their marriage made it. In fact, they more than made it. These days, the two of them are about one of the happiest couples you'd ever want to meet.

That's one of the reasons they share a passion for mentoring couples who've been through similar circumstances. And, boy, do they work as a team!

It's very clear that one of Jeff's strengths is to pull no punches in making sure that a mentoree couple is shooting straight with them. Melinda tends to cringe when confrontation enters a conversation but she knows it's occasionally necessary for the kind of mentoring they do. "Truth is, if Jeff didn't drill down on the heart of the matter sometimes," she confesses, "I'm not sure we'd make much progress with our mentorees." On the other hand, Jeff steps back and lets Melinda take the lead when it comes to gently focusing on what's necessary for healing to take place. In short, they know each other's strengths.

One of the other ways they work as a team is to echo each other's points. It's never blatant, but it's enough to let their mentorees know they are together on something. For example, in a recent session Melinda made the point that forgiving your spouse is not only beneficial to your marriage but to you as an individual. Jeff underscored this by relaying the difference forgiveness not only made to them as a couple but what it did for his own spirit and outlook.

And, of course, Jeff and Melinda are quite adept at embracing their differences. They even joke about it in front of their mentorees. "I learned a long time ago that Melinda likes to air out any suspicious thoughts she might have about me," says Jeff. "I don't like it after all these years—but I understand it and I embrace it." He goes on to say that he actually respects her for doing what she does when it's not his style or desire. "That's part of what makes marriage interesting." And it's part of what makes their mentoring sessions interesting and effective as well—because they work as a team.

CHAPTER 11

AGREEING ON OUTCOMES

We should all be concerned about the future
because we will have to spend the rest of our lives there.
CHARLES F. KETTERING

You're on your way to a new location when you begin wondering whether your husband is driving in the right direction.

"Does this seem right to you?" you ask him gently.

"I'm not sure, but let's see what's up the road a bit," he replies, rather more brusquely.

"Why don't we ask for directions?" you say, frustration growing.

And that's when your husband begins to drive faster, right? "I know where I'm going," he will say, as if he's suddenly tuned into an internal gyrocompass that only he can read.

When you step back from the situation, you'll realize you've arrived at one of the prototypical marriage moments that define all couples. You both know the experience; we've all lived it. And more than likely we will repeat it many times. But when it comes to setting out on the metaphorical journey of marriage mentoring, we can't afford to wander without a true and clear sense of direction. That's why we focus this chapter on helping you find your way along the mentoring path.

What does it mean to agree on outcomes? It means being proactive about where you'd like to be as two couples in a mentoring relationship when you have completed your work. It means getting specific and charting your course. Far too many couples ride like passengers on a bumpy bus, watching the scenery flash by their window as life passes by. Not marriage mentors, however.

We'll be honest. Agreeing on outcomes is not always easy. It requires initiative. It requires your mentorees to take responsibility for their marriage. 119

After all, you can't do the work for them. You are mentors, not mothers. Make no mistake, your mentorees will never achieve their ideal marriage as mere passengers; they must have their collective hand on the wheel.

> *Love does not consist in gazing at each other but in looking together in the same direction.*
> ANTOINE DE SAINT-EXUPÉRY

In his play *Don Juan in Hell*, George Bernard Shaw correctly concluded: "Hell is to drift, heaven is to steer." This marriage mentor skill is dedicated to helping you show your mentorees how to steer their marriage in the direction of heaven on earth. And it begins with prayerfully thinking about what needs to happen while seeking God's direction.

"IF YOU COULD PRESS A MAGIC BUTTON ..."

Here's a question we've probably asked every couple we've ever mentored: If you could press a magic button, what would you like to instantly make different in your marriage? If they are stuck, we may give them some suggestions. Perhaps they'd like to enjoy more romance. Maybe they'd like to have fewer quarrels. Would they prefer to have more meals as a family with the television off? Every couple has things they'd like to change.

You may even want to have your mentorees make a list of a half-dozen things they wish were different. You can have them do this separately and then compare notes. You might even have them spend some time with you processing these items and prioritizing them together. Why? Because this will serve as a springboard for setting goals that will help them improve their relationship.

SET OBJECTIVE AND ATTAINABLE GOALS

Henry Ford said, "You can't build a reputation on what you are going to do." That's true. But if you are going to do something that eventually does build your reputation and leave a legacy, you must chart your course of action by setting a few goals.

Obviously, this is something you want to do early on with any mentoree couple you meet with. Knowing your objectives gives everyone a purpose and a sense of comfort. It provides direction for you and your mentorees. And truth be told, they probably haven't thought much about their goals. Most couples don't. Only a small fraction have ever put their goals in writing. Are those who don't missing out? Absolutely. Research reveals that simply having a list of goals in your possession dramatically increases your chances of reaching your goals. Not only that, people who make a tangible list and keep it handy are far more likely to achieve their goals than others who have the very same desires.

Whether you are mentoring an engaged couple, a couple wanting to move from good to great, or a couple in distress, take time early on to discuss their goals. Write them down. Have them do the same. Decide on a place where they can keep them visible. Both partners need to see them several times throughout the week.

BE SURE THE GOALS ALIGN WITH GOD'S PURPOSE

Matt Emmons had the gold medal in sight. He was one shot away from claiming victory in the 2004 Olympic 50-meter three-position rifle event. He didn't even need a bull's-eye to win. His final shot merely needed to be on target.

Normally, the shot he made would have received a score of 8.1, more than enough for a gold medal. But in what was described as "an extremely rare mistake in elite competition," Emmons fired at the wrong target. Standing in lane two, he fired at the target in lane three. His score for a good shot at the wrong target? Zero. Instead of a medal, Emmons ended up in eighth place.

The point? It doesn't matter how accurate you are if you are aiming at the wrong goal. As you help your mentorees craft their goals for their marriage, be sure to seek God's guidance. Pray together as couples that this goal-setting process would honor Christ. Pray that God would reveal his desires during this time you share together. If your mentorees' goal is to build a big house and buy a yacht, for example, it may be good to gently explore the spiritual purpose. Never make them feel guilty for their goals, but help them consider how their goals align with God's purpose for their lives together.

Some mentorees, on the other hand, can't seem to set their sights high enough. Their goals are, well, mediocre. You'll want to help them lift their vision. C. S. Lewis, in his sermon "The Weight of Glory," said, "Our Lord finds our desires not too strong, but too weak. We are half-hearted creatures, too easily pleased."

Bottom line, be sure that whatever goals your couple is cultivating are in tune with biblical understanding.

UNDERSCORE THE DREADED D-WORD

In his compelling book *Me: The Narcissistic American*, psychoanalyst Aaron Stern gets right to the point: "To attain emotional maturity, each of us must learn to develop ... the ability to delay immediate gratification in favor of long-range goals."

That's the key. Delayed gratification. Or, if you prefer, discipline. It makes most of us cringe. But the beauty of this sometimes-elusive qual-ity of character is that it becomes more abun-dant in marriage. After all, we have a built-in accountability partner in our spouse. Whether it's including regular exercise into our schedule, keeping a tidy house, taming our tongues, or being consistent in prayer, our spouse can play a vital role in encouraging us and keeping us accountable.

> *God never put anyone in a place too small to grow.*
>
> HENRIETTA MEARS

This aspect of a couple's accountability to each other is worth noting to your mentorees. Not only that, but when they realize they have marriage mentors investing in them to help them reach their goals, the chances of attaining those goals become even more likely. That's good news. The dread of "discipline" isn't so bad after all!

STOP AND SMELL THE ROSES

Architect Frank Lloyd Wright once told of an incident that seemed insig-nificant at the time but had a profound influence on the rest of his life. The winter he was nine, he went walking across a snow-covered field with his reserved, no-nonsense uncle. As the two of them reached the far end of the field, his uncle stopped him. He pointed out his own tracks in the snow, straight and true as an arrow's flight, and then young Frank's tracks meandering all over the field. "Notice how your tracks wander aimlessly from the fence to the cattle to the woods and back again," his uncle said. "And see how my tracks aim directly to my goal. There is an important lesson in that."

Years later the world-famous architect liked to tell how this experience had greatly contributed to his philosophy in life. "I determined right then," he'd say with a twinkle in his eye, "not to miss most things in life, as my uncle had."

It's a good lesson. One that is worth learning right from the start as you are crafting a set of goals with your mentorees. You don't want to be so focused on the task of compulsively achieving a goal that you miss out on the spontaneity of a moment that offers more joy than completing the task. In other words, as marriage mentors who may be working with a hard-driving mentoree couple, never hesitate to stop and smell the proverbial roses. And if your mentorees are really unbalanced, you might even need to suggest to them (or maybe just the husband) to have a "goal" of relaxing and doing nothing.

GET SPECIFIC ON WHAT YOU CAN COMMIT TO

Let's get to one of the nitty-gritty aspects of marriage mentoring. You only have so much time, right? Whether you have a full-time job and a busy family or you are retired and making your own schedule, your time for marriage mentoring is limited. So what are the limits? How many hours per month are you willing to give it? Get specific.

This, of course, is a discussion for just the two of you to explore. You need to be honest with each other and set your limits right from the beginning. How often and when can you meet your mentorees? Do you want to meet them in your own home? In theirs? Maybe you'd prefer to meet over a meal at a quiet restaurant. For how many sessions can you meet? Do you want to be finished by a certain date? The more specific you can be about what you would like the structure of this time to look like, the better. Why? Because then you can let your mentorees know the boundaries. You'll avoid any unspoken disappointment — on your side as well as theirs.

We suggest you do this before your first meeting with your mentorees for obvious reasons. And we place this suggestion in this chapter because it may influence the kind of goals you will set with your mentorees. For example, maybe you are only willing to mentor them for six months before taking a sabbatical from your work and doing some extensive traveling. This will preclude you working with them on goals that may extend beyond this time period. You get the idea. Just be clear about expectations from the start and you'll save yourself some heartache down the road.

PRACTICE AND PROMISE CONFIDENTIALITY

Confidentiality is so important that it almost should go without saying, but we don't want to risk it. What takes place between you and your mentorees is private information and they need to know that. If they suspect that you might be leaking their secrets to their pastor, parents, or friends—or even to total strangers—the mentoring relationship will never get to a deep and meaningful level. There is no justifiable excuse for inadvertent slips that reveal private information shared with you in confidence.

We know a then-engaged couple, for example, who had a great rapport with their marriage mentors. The only drawback from the couple's point of view was how one of the mentors often talked specifically—without intending to gossip, mind you—about other couples whom they had prepared for marriage. As they all went to the same church, this broke the rules of confidentiality and resulted in the fact that the mentorees didn't fully trust the mentors. They weren't willing to share their deepest fears, dreams, or past hurts because they didn't want them "unintentionally" spread around the church.

> *A gossip betrays a confidence, but a trustworthy man keeps a secret.*
>
> PROVERBS 11:13

But are there times when you need to break a confidence? Sure. Whenever someone's safety is in jeopardy, if abuse is taking place, or suicide is a risk. Of course, these scenarios are very rare in a mentoring relationship. Couples struggling with such profoundly devastating issues are more likely to be seeing a professional counselor already (or need to).

KEEP THE BIG PICTURE IN MIND

In the movie *The Bridge on the River Kwai*, the lead character, Colonel Nicholson, is a prisoner of war in Burma who leads his men to build a bridge for his Japanese captors. Nicholson is an officer of high integrity, dedicated to excellence, a great leader of men—and thus well trained to complete any mission that he is given. He builds a beautiful bridge.

By the film's end, he finds himself in the painful position of defending the bridge from attack by fellow officers who want to destroy it to prevent Japanese trains from using it. There's a chilling moment of realization, right before he detonates the bridge, when Nicholson utters the famous line, "What have I done?" He was so focused on his goal—building the bridge—that he forgot the larger mission of winning the war.

It's a good lesson for every marriage mentor couple who is helping their mentorees agree on some tangible outcomes. Sure, you've noted some specific goals. You've outlined some specific steps. But don't forget what it's all about. In chapter 3 we noted the definition of marriage mentoring as:

a relatively happy, more experienced couple purposefully investing in another couple to effectively navigate a journey that they have already taken. Keeping this definition in mind, or your adaptation of it, will help you stay focused on the big picture.

Max DePree, former CEO of Herman Miller, Inc., is a master of keeping the big picture in mind. He writes: "It is not a matter primarily of whether or not we reach our particular goals. Life is more than just reaching our goals. As individuals and as a group we need to reach our potential. We must always be reaching toward our potential."[1]

Charles Conn has a different way of underscoring this point: "Looking through a peephole is no way to stay motivated when you're moving toward a goal. The big view is important. It takes big dreams—big goals, big faith—to keep us moving through obstacles and fatigue and discouragement."[2]

Maintaining momentum in marriage mentoring requires constantly reminding ourselves what we are working toward. Remembering the big picture always makes the smaller goals more attainable.

The Minimal Outcomes

Not every mentor couple is comfortable with specific outcomes. Just how detailed you like to get with this is up to you. But experience has shown that the most effective mentoring work does articulate a few minimal agreements. These are mutually agreed upon ways of structuring your mentoring process that typically emerge in a discussion between both you and your mentorees, recognizing that you as the mentors will have more wisdom in shaping the expectations. Here are some minimal suggestions:

- What topics should we cover? You may want to note two or three specific items.

- When will we start and when will we end the formal mentoring process? This doesn't mean the relationship has to end at that point (formally or informally); it simply provides a predetermined point at which to reexamine the relationship in light of any new circumstances.

- How often will we meet and for how long in each session? This may be predetermined by your schedule and timeline but it should be something that is clear to both couples.

- How will you know when you are making progress? This makes the outcomes of your mentoring meetings more tangible and definable.

We've focused on some important skills for the mentoring relationship. Let's turn in the next few chapters to those based on how you will interact with your mentorees, namely related to questions, answers, and stories.

REAL-LIFE EXAMPLE OF *Agreeing on Outcomes*

Jerry was always a little too driven. As the owner of his own chain of carpet stores in his state, he more or less had to be. He set goals at work and he worked hard to reach them. And he was a master at delayed gratification. The problem? His driven nature didn't always jibe with Shannon's. Let's rephrase that. It hardly ever was in sync with Shannon. They were happily married but if Jerry ran on high octane, Shannon only required regular.

So when Jerry and Shannon, married twenty-six years, decided to volunteer as marriage mentors at their church, it was no big surprise to Shannon that Jerry took charge. In their first meeting with their mentoree couple, Jerry was eager to nail down the goal. He wanted to zero in on every problem and set a measurable timeline for solving it.

Needless to say, this didn't work too well. Jerry's intentions were good but he needed to ease off the gas pedal and proceed a bit more slowly. And he did. With the help of some mentor training and by paying more attention to Shannon's cues, Jerry learned to harness his inclination and use it when the time was right. After building a sense of rapport, for example. And after spending some time allowing his mentorees to reveal what was really going on for them.

Jerry and Shannon are now experts at helping mentorees agree on outcomes. Recently they worked with a younger couple who wanted to improve their relationships with their in-laws, especially on the husband's side. A worthy goal indeed. One of the first steps was to make this goal a little more concrete.

"What would your relationship look like with your in-laws if it was improved?" Shannon asked the couple.

"I think we'd just be more relaxed together around them," the young bride answered.

"Do you agree?" Jerry asked the new husband.

Both agreed that this would be a desirable outcome. But as Jerry and Shannon began to clarify this issue further, they realized that the uneasiness this couple was experiencing with their in-laws really had more to do with how the new husband was ignoring his bride whenever they were with his parents. As this became apparent to Jerry and Shannon and as they in turn shared this perspective with their mentorees, the couple willingly shifted their desired outcome of the mentoring sessions to how they acted *as a new husband and wife* when they were together with his parents.

By exploring outcomes with this couple, Jerry and Shannon were able to get to the more accurate source of the issue and work on it. Think of the time that was saved in this mentoring relationship by taking a few minutes to agree on outcomes.

CHAPTER 12

ASKING MEANINGFUL QUESTIONS

You can make more friends in two months by becoming interested
in other people than you can in two years by trying to get other people
interested in you.
DALE CARNEGIE

Asking meaningful questions. This skill is among the most important to
hone as a marriage mentor. Its impact, if not consciously studied, causes it
to go unnoticed because it all too often is taken for granted. But once you
recognize its power, you will never approach your mentoring relationships
without it.

The grandfather of all people-skills books was published in 1937 and
was an overnight hit, eventually selling 15 million copies. *How to Win
Friends and Influence People* by Dale Carnegie is just as useful today as it
was when it was first published, because Dale Carnegie had an understanding of human nature that will never be outdated. The skills he teaches in
this classic book are undergirded by a pervasive principle: people crave to
be known and appreciated.

Quality questions are intentionally designed to open up a person's
spirit. They aren't throwaway questions like "How about those Red Sox?"
or "Can you believe this weather?" — though that type of nonthreatening
opener certainly has its place.

Quality questions invite vulnerability, but are not invasive. They are
personal, but respect privacy. They are asked out of genuine interest, but
are never blunt. A quality question conveys kindness, warmth, concern,
and interest. It is couched in affirmation and appreciation.

Perhaps you are already a pro at asking quality questions. Terrific! But
if you are like most people, you could probably benefit from getting a bit of
a brushup in this area. So let's take a look at how this works.   129

THE POWER OF A QUALITY QUESTION

Consider a simple example that does not specifically relate to marriage mentoring. We were speaking in Chicago and the host couple assigned to pick us up at O'Hare Airport was waiting outside security with our names on a placard. "Welcome to Illinois, I'm Philip and this is my wife Cara," he said as he reached to carry a suitcase or two. We hopped in their vehicle and were on our way — until we hit rush-hour traffic. We were at a near standstill for almost an hour and that gave us plenty of time to talk.

"Tell us about your hobbies. What do you do for fun?" I (Les) asked them.

Philip became animated as he told us about their new boat. Soon Cara jumped in and began talking about how much fun they have together on the water.

"Sounds like you really enjoy it," Leslie followed up, "and I bet you work hard to maintain it."

"Oh yes," Cara replied. "It can be a little time-consuming but it's worth it." She went on to describe a vacation they had planned which included a lot of water skiing.

"You really love it, don't you?" we said.

"It's not only fun, you get a lot of exercise too." Philip then told us about his father's triple bypass surgery two years ago.

As the traffic crawled, we asked Philip and Cara about their kids. That's when they told us about their struggle with infertility and how they had their first child just two years ago. "Her name is Rigby."

"I bet there's a story behind that name," Leslie said.

Cara got a photo out of her purse and began to tell us how the name came about.

"You must feel so blessed to have this little girl," we said.

"God's timing is amazing. In fact, the same month she was born I got a new job closer to home," Philip said. Cara piped in to tell us how they are working on the pervasive problem of managing their busy lives.

With traffic still bottlenecked and time on our hands, we asked Cara more about that: "When do you two have your best moments together as a couple?" They had to ponder that for a moment but then began telling us how they sometimes feel they give everyone else their best time and the two of them simply get what's leftover. We commiserated with them on that and then Cara said, "We've never really told anyone this, but about a year before Rigby was born we wondered whether we were actually going to make it." They told us about going to counseling and what they had learned. Suddenly we were oceans deep into their marriage. They confided in us about several sensitive issues in their marriage and we simply and gently asked quality questions.

When we finally pulled up to the hotel and were unloading our bags, Philip asked us each for our calling card and said, "You two sure are interesting; it was great getting to know you."

"It sure was," Cara chimed in. And with that Philip and Cara climbed into their SUV and sped away. We looked at each other and smiled.

Truth be told, Philip and Cara didn't get to know us at all. In an hour of conversation, they literally did not ask a single question with the exception of the obligatory, "How was your flight?" We're sad to say that it's not an uncommon experience. Many people don't know how to put the spotlight on the people they are with. They've never consciously considered how to pull a person out and make them feel known.

The only reason Philip and Cara thought we were interesting is because we showed genuine interest in them. And we affirmed them on top of it. For a whole hour, they were on center stage with two strangers who were both supplying them with a string of quality questions about themselves.

PUTTING THE FOCUS ON YOUR MENTOREES

As you consider the experience we had with Philip and Cara, notice that we said next to nothing about ourselves. This wasn't by design. In fact, we would have preferred that the conversation go both ways. But it didn't. Had we been together over more time, the chances of a more equal give and take may have occurred, but that's not guaranteed. Some people, and couples, simply don't know how to follow a line of questioning that naturally allows another person to be known. People just don't think about it. That's why so many conversations are characterized as "small talk." People don't get to the big issues, the more meaningful issues, because they don't ask meaningful questions.

> *It is better to know some of the questions than all of the answers.*
> JAMES THURBER

This can't be the case for marriage mentors. As imbalanced as this may seem on occasion, it rests with you to carry the conversation. This doesn't mean you do most of the talking. It means you do most of the questioning and reflecting. In an upcoming chapter on listening we will provide more information on how to do this effectively, but our point here is that the focus of the conversation should be on your mentorees. And almost always, the more you can get them to talk about themselves, the better.

Perhaps you are already well aware of the power of this simple strategy. Maybe you have been doing it intuitively for years. Congratulations. We are sure you don't lack for friends. But if you are unsure, or if you sometimes endure too many conversational lulls or feel socially awkward in the mentoring process it's probably due to your lack of asking meaningful questions.

How to Ask a Meaningful Line of Questions

Our friend John Maxwell has written many helpful books on leadership. As a pastor, and now as an internationally known speaker and author, John encounters a lot of people. And he has a reputation for winning with people. One day we asked John to reveal some of his secrets. "For me, it comes down to asking another person a good question." He went on to tell us that over the years he had developed a list of six questions that have helped him in this endeavor time and time again. Here they are:

1. *"What do you dream about?"*
   To understand the mind of people look at what they have already achieved. To understand the heart of people look at what they dream of becoming.

2. *"What do you cry about?"*
   When you know where people carry their pain, what makes them hurt, you can't help but understand their heart.

3. *"What do you sing about?"*
   When you know what brings joy to people, you know where they draw their strength.

4. *"What are your values?"*
   If you can identify people's values, you have entered the most sacred chambers of their heart.

5. *"What are your strengths?"*
   Once you understand how people perceive their strengths, you understand what makes their hearts proud.

6. *"What is your temperament?"*
   When you discover people's personality traits, you discover the uniqueness of their heart's hardwiring.

Of course, this is not a "to-do" list of questions that you need to ask your mentorees, but it gives you an idea of the different lines of questioning that may be fruitful.

> *The important thing is not to stop questioning.*
> ALBERT EINSTEIN

Perhaps the most important key to asking good questions is found in the fact that some of the best "questions" aren't really questions at all. They are statements that welcome a person to share their heart. "Sounds like this is important to you," for example. Or, "I'm guessing you have some feelings about that." These kinds of statements following a mentoree's comments can do wonders for opening their spirit.

Here's the bottom line to asking quality questions. As you think in terms of the big question—"How is this couple doing?"—and as you choose to be genuinely interested in the answer, you will witness how easily and naturally a line of quality questions flows.

THE MASTER QUESTIONER

When it comes to asking meaningful questions, we would be remiss if we did not note that this was one of Jesus' primary means of connecting with others. You might find it helpful to spend some time looking at the questions Jesus used when he worked with people. For example, consider these:

Question	Person(s) Being Asked	Scripture Reference
"Which is easier: to say to the paralytic, 'Your sins are forgiven,' or to say, 'Get up, take your mat and walk'?"	Teachers of the law at a home in Capernaum	Mark 2:1–12 (v. 9)
"Why are you so afraid?"	Disciples in boat	Mark 4:35–41 (v. 40)
"What is your name?"	Possessed man	Mark 5:1–20 (v. 9)
"Who touched me?"	Sick woman	Mark 5:21–34 (v. 31)
"Why all this commotion and wailing?"	Grieving people	Mark 5:35–43 (v. 39)
"Don't you see …?"	Disciples in house	Mark 7:17–23 (v. 18)
"What did Moses command you?"	Pharisees	Mark 10:1–11 (v. 3)
"Why do you call me good?"	Rich young man	Mark 10:17–22 (v. 18)
"Why are you bothering her?"	People at party	Mark 14:1–9 (v. 6)
"Are you asleep? Could you not keep watch for one hour?"	Peter, James, and John in garden	Mark 14:35–41 (vv. 37, 41)

This is only a small sampling of questions Jesus raised as recorded in Mark's gospel. Out of sixty-seven episodes in which Jesus has any sort of conversation, fifty of those contain Jesus' questions (and that's omitting double questions).[1] Reading through the texts and reflecting on them may provide you with some insight into how Jesus effectively raised questions.

> *Apparently if you met Jesus on the street, he was more likely to ask you something than to tell you something.*
> CONRAD GEMPF

You notice that he didn't ask rhetorical questions that call for no answers. Rather his inquiries seemed designed to involve people. He used questions to help people draw conclusions and to correct their thinking. Often instead of answering his own questions he used them to lead his listeners toward truth. He was not hesitant to ask direct and probing questions, yet he did so with a love for the individual.

One moving example of this is the interview Jesus conducted in the Samaritan village of Sychar. As he speaks with the Samaritan woman he skillfully draws her out by asking "Will you give me a drink?" (John 4:7). This leads to a productive conversation that shows compassion, balance, and a sensitivity to the woman's background and needs—all qualities worth cultivating in our questions with couples. We would do well to study and imitate the example of Christ and allow that to shape the way we interact with our mentorees.

If you are successful in asking provocative questions you will open up a torrent of responses. When that happens you'll need to know how to listen aggressively. Let's look at that in the next chapter.

Asking Meaningful Questions

Russ and Joleen, marriage mentors in Denver, Colorado, have learned to field all sorts of questions from their mentorees. One couple in particular gave them many challenges—and many laughs. After many years of single life, these two people married and found several unexpected potholes on the road to blending their lives as husband and wife.

In one of their mentoring sessions, Russ and Joleen learned that their mentorees were having heated arguments over shoes in the house. You see, this mentoree couple began their married life together in *her* house; and in *her* house, she kept a tray by the door for shoes. The custom upon entering the house was to put your shoes in the tray. In all his life to that point, the husband had never taken his shoes off before entering his house. So naturally, he simply walked right past the tray (not knowing what it was for) and plopped himself into a chair in the living room. After nagging at him for weeks, she finally exploded, accusing him of having no respect for her or the house she had cared for long before they got married.

"How do I fix this?" the husband asked Russ while their wives were getting some goodies in the kitchen.

"Well," asked Russ in return, "do you still walk into the house with your shoes on?"

"Yeah," he replied.

"Have you tried to talk to her about it?"

"No."

"Seems that might be a good idea! Maybe you could ask her when she comes back."

So, a humbled husband asked his new wife why she wanted the shoes in the tray. After learning how important it was to her, he determined to put his shoes in the tray. And she, after learning how challenging it was for him to remember (after a lifetime of doing otherwise), determined to overlook the times that he forgot.

The solution to their problem began with a simple question: "Have you tried to talk to her about it?" Not all simple questions can lead to such quick success, but as Russ and Joleen will testify, a good question can take marriage mentors a long way toward helping other couples.

CHAPTER 13

LISTENING AGGRESSIVELY

The best way to persuade is with your ears.

DEAN RUSK

As one of the youngest commanding officers in the Navy's Pacific Fleet, Michael Abrashoff took command of his first ship and wasted no time instituting radical changes. Antiquated, do-as-I-say leadership practices literally went overboard when Mike stepped aboard the *USS Benfold* and began practicing what he calls "aggressive listening." In his book *It's Your Ship*, Captain Abrashoff explains what he means:

> It didn't take me long to realize that my young crew was smart, talented, and full of good ideas that frequently came to nothing because no one in charge had ever listened to them. Like most organizations, the Navy seemed to put managers in a transmitting mode, which minimized their receptivity. They were conditioned to promulgate orders from above, not to welcome suggestions from below.
>
> I decided that my job was to listen aggressively and to pick up every good idea the crew had for improving the ship's operation. Some traditionalists might consider this heresy, but it's actually just common sense. After all, the people who do the nuts-and-bolts work on a ship constantly see things that officers don't. It seemed to me only prudent for the captain to work hard at seeing the ship through the crew's eyes. Something happened in me as a result of those interviews. I came to respect my crew enormously. No longer were they nameless bodies at which I barked orders. I realized that they ... had hopes, dreams, loved ones, and they wanted to believe that what they were doing was important. And they wanted to be treated with respect.[1]

That's the power of listening. Like empathy, it can change you. Aggressive listening opens up a window into another person's life and allows you to see them like you never have before.

If listening can be powerful enough to transform a naval ship, just think what it can do for a marriage mentoring relationship. This is, without a doubt, an essential skill for every marriage mentor. And, by the way, it's been in practice long before Captain Abrashoff wrote about it.

Effective listening requires more than hearing the words transmitted. It demands that you find meaning and understanding in what is being said. After all, meanings are not in words, but in people.

HERB COHEN

Anyone who has studied the Bible has seen the power of listening in action. Even as a young boy Jesus was sitting with the teachers in the temple, "listening to them and asking them questions [and] everyone ... was amazed at his understanding" (Luke 2:46–47). The apostle Paul understood that listening requires diligent work. When he was before Agrippa, he said, "I beg you to listen to me patiently" (Acts 26:3). The book of James tells us to "be quick to listen [and] slow to speak" (1:19). And the book of Proverbs says: "He who answers before listening—that is his folly and his shame" (18:13). The word *listen* occurs over two hundred times in the Bible.

So what does a marriage mentor need to know about active listening? First of all, you need to unplug your ears. (We'll explain that in a moment!) You also need to listen to understand. And most importantly, you need to listen for feelings. This is the essence of active listening. Let's explore each of these.

GET YOUR EARS UNPLUGGED

Before you attempt to master any other listening skill, you must first eliminate all the potential barriers on the roadway to effective listening:

Distractions—Telephone, television, pager, and all the rest. If you want to truly listen, you have to remove these distractions.

Defensiveness—If you perceive any particular comment as a criticism, you are likely to get defensive. And that shuts down listening.

Closed-mindedness—Unwillingness to consider the opinions and ideas of others will obviously shut your ears. If you've already made up your mind and closed the case, you'll never truly listen.

Projection—Attributing your own thoughts and feelings to another person spells disaster. Once you lose objectivity and believe "he's the one who's angry," when you're the one who is actually hot under the collar, you'll never hear what's being said.

Assumption—Drawing conclusions about the meaning or intention of what is said before you truly understand it will quickly terminate listening. Whenever you jump to conclusions, you convey a message that you aren't even interested.

Pride—Thinking you have little to learn from your mentorees will prevent you from listening. This is, perhaps, the most deadly of distractions to active listening. You'll never unplug your ears if your head is full of yourself.

LISTEN TO UNDERSTAND

The fundamental cause of almost all communication problems is that people do not listen to understand—they listen to reply. To listen within the frame of reference of the other person is the key to both understanding and influence as a marriage mentor.

David Burns, a medical doctor and professor of psychiatry at the University of Pennsylvania, says: "The biggest mistake you can make in trying to talk convincingly is to put your highest priority on expressing your ideas and feelings. What most people really want is to be listened to, respected, and understood." And what Dr. Burns says next is a valuable insight: "The moment people see that they are being understood, they become more motivated to understand your point of view."

> *Listen or thy tongue will keep thee deaf.*
> AMERICAN INDIAN
> PROVERB

If you have any experience in marriage mentoring you know this is true. As a mentoree couple feels understood by you, they are certain to open up their spirits. They will welcome your influence and input.

LISTEN FOR FEELINGS

In between what a person intends to communicate and what others hear stands an unavoidable filter of preconception. The discouraged wife who says, "I'm not going to waste my time trying to do a budget with him" may mean, "I am too embarrassed to tell you that I feel inadequate about how I spend money." The hurting couple who says, "We just don't have any time to have a date night" may mean, "I'm afraid we wouldn't have anything to talk about if it was just the two of us." Or the suspicious husband who asks a marriage mentor, "Do you really think so?" may mean, "I disagree with you."

A mentor can target three aspects of a given message from a mentoree by reflecting: (1) the content of the message, (2) the thinking behind the message, and (3) the feeling behind the message. Each is equally valid and useful. To help you better understand what is meant by *reflecting*, here is an example of how a single statement may be reflected at each level.

WIFE: I couldn't believe he was accusing me for what *he* did.
MENTOR REFLECTING CONTENT: He blamed you.
WIFE: Yes. He said I was the one responsible because I was there.
MENTOR REFLECTING THINKING: You thought he was unfair.
WIFE: Yes. I didn't deserve to be blamed.
MENTOR REFLECTING FEELING: It must have made you angry.
WIFE: I was furious. I also felt bad.

By reflecting the content of the message, the mentor allows the mentoree to elaborate further on what happened. By reflecting the thinking behind the message, the mentor allows the mentoree to understand her evaluation of what happened. And by reflecting the feeling behind the message, the mentor invites the mentoree to become aware of her emotions as a result of what happened, which is often the most revealing aspect of all.

Here are a couple more examples:

HUSBAND: I didn't know how she would respond to me wanting her to take more responsibility for the budget, but she was very eager to do it.
MENTOR REFLECTING FEELING: You must be happy.
HUSBAND: I was really relieved. It feels great.

WIFE: We thought setting up our home would be fun, but it turned into a minor disaster when we couldn't agree on where to place a single picture.
MENTOR REFLECTING FEELING: Sounds frustrating.
WIFE: It was. You could cut the tension with a knife. Fortunately, we eventually got over it and finally got our act together.

By reflecting the feelings of a newlywed, we are not evaluating or advising. We are saying "I am with you and want to understand you better." Reflecting your mentoree's feeling may not seem like much to offer, but it is more than a married couple will get from nearly anyone else.

Useful Leads for the Active Listener

It sounds like you're feeling ...	It seems as if ...
I get a picture of ...	What I hear you saying is ...
Could it be that ...	It must have been ...
I'm wondering if you're thinking ...	You must feel...

WHAT ACTIVE LISTENING DOES FOR YOUR MENTOREES

If you've ever worked to listen aggressively, if you've disciplined yourself to actively listen to the message beneath the words, you know it's not easy. It takes a continual, conscious effort. But we think it is so worth it. The rewards for your mentoring relationship are plentiful; let's take a look.

Listening Unearths Hidden Feelings

Active listing allows a mentoree's hidden feelings to percolate to the top. Unless they are at a point of real crisis, couples do not often broadcast their pain. They want someone to sense their hurt without them having to admit it. Their anxiety about a particular circumstance, for example, sometimes hides behind a smiling face.

To help your mentorees, you need a sensitive, internal seismograph to feel the subterranean tremors underneath the external calm. In effect, that is what active listening is—a way to sense the inevitable quakings of a marriage. If you have a hunch that a wife is not as apathetic as she seems, but actually angry because her husband isn't as sensitive as she once thought, don't blurt out: "You are denying how angry you really are." Instead you may probe gently: "Something about the way you're talking gives me the sense that you might be angry but feel you're not supposed to be." A statement like this allows the wife to own her buried disappointment without losing face. It unearths the hidden feelings that might otherwise remain buried.

> *Difficult as it is really to listen to someone in affliction, it is just as difficult for him to know that compassion is listening to him.*
> SIMONE WEIL

Listening Takes Away the Fear of Feeling

Free from evaluation, active listening creates a safe environment. It provides a place where a trembling couple can shed defenses and own up to previously feared emotions. It allows them to say their feelings are accept-able. When mentorees are guarded, it is like they are holding the accelera-tor all the way down but keeping the car in neutral and their foot on the brake—using valuable fuel (like your time) and going nowhere. Active listening can give mentorees new energy and help them move in a positive direction.

Listening Helps Couples Grow

The marriage mentor's goal is not to be depended upon. Mentor-ing isn't rescuing. Too often we mistake help with throwing out a line of advice. The problem with solving a couple's problems is that external solutions foster unhealthy dependence. If you solve a problem for a couple who comes back repeatedly with a similar problem, you are putting out the same fire over and over. When we *listen* to mentorees, we are in effect say-ing, "I believe in you and your marriage," while *giving advice* says, "I don't trust you to come up with your own solution." Active listening boosts the confidence of newlyweds and teaches them to depend on God and them-selves for problem solving.

Now that the conversation with your mentorees is moving forward as you ask provocative questions and listen actively, you probably won't be sur-prised that things will soon go deep. And that the discussion might throw up questions that you never anticipated having to answer. Let's see how to field the unexpected question in chapter 14.

REAL-LIFE EXAMPLE OF *Listening Aggressively*

Reggie and Tina, married fifteen years, learned the hard way how valuable aggressive listening is to marriage mentoring. "When we first started as mentors," says Reggie, "I thought the goal was to help the mentorees solve problems. I thought that if I wasn't fixing something for them then I wasn't being a good mentor."

A mentoree couple in their care began talking about how one of them was more controlling with money than the other. They were recounting a conflict they had in the grocery story over whether they could afford certain items or not. Ding, ding, ding. This was Reggie's cue to jump in and tell them how to correct the situation. Funny thing is, when Reggie did this, the mentorees simply clammed up whenever he started in on one of his monologues about how they should do this or that.

With some basic marriage mentor training and a little more experience, however, Reggie did an about-face. He began to bite his tongue when he could feel himself gearing up with trigger-happy advice. And Tina, with a gentle touch on his knee, helped him to remember to listen instead of lecture. And that's just what he did. In fact, Reggie began to listen so well during their mentoring sessions, Tina began to joke with him that she'd like to see him do half that much listening when it's just the two of them at home.

"I've gotten so much better," says Reggie. "Now, when a mentoree couple tells me about a conflict they are having, I don't try to immediately fix the situation. Instead, I make sure I genuinely understand them. I gently probe with a few questions. I hold back on advice and listen for their feelings."

"It's true," says Tina. "He's really good at this now."

"I almost feel like a detective sometimes, like Columbo, just asking questions and waiting for the true feelings in the couple to emerge. It's actually fun," Reggie says.

And once the feelings emerge? "It's amazing how often the problem solves itself," he says with enthusiasm. "These kids think we're geniuses with all kinds of wisdom when all we are really doing is listening!"

"But don't kid yourself," says Tina, "listening like this takes work. That's why it's so special and helpful to our mentorees."

CHAPTER 14

FIELDING ANY QUESTION THEY THROW AT YOU

Man will not live without answers to his questions.
HANS J. MORTENTHAU

Early in his career, A. J. Jacobs put his Ivy League education to work at *Entertainment Weekly*, a magazine devoted to stories of media celebrities and reviews. He emerged five years later realizing he wanted to put his brain to work on something more challenging. So he set off on a quest to read the entire contents of the *Encyclopedia Britannica*, all thirty-three thousand pages, all forty-four million words.

The mission began in October 2002, with the first page of volume one of the thirty-two–volume set. As Jacobs recounted, "I wanted to be able to answer almost any question that was thrown at me." So he filled his head with useful and less-useful knowledge. And some years later he wrote a book about his quest called *The Know-It-All*, in which he reveals his obsession for learning and his effort at hard-won wisdom.

Sometimes we have the sneaking suspicion that some marriage mentors are a little like A. J. Jacobs. We fear they feel a compulsive need to know everything about marriage if they are to be effective mentors. But they don't.

Over the years, as we've recruited couples to be marriage mentors, they often say, "We don't know how to mentor." Or they tell us that their marriage isn't all it could be. Or that they don't have the time. We have heard dozens of seemingly good reasons for not being marriage mentors, but far and away, the most common reason potential marriage mentors give for not volunteering is that they don't have all the answers. "I don't know what I'd say if they asked me something about budgets, or in-laws, or (yikes!) sex."

So let's say it straight: marriage mentors aren't expected to have "all the answers." Whew!

Take a deep breath. Relax. You don't have to stay up reading marriage encyclopedias. You don't have to earn an advanced degree in marriage therapy. You simply need to be you — and to know the one answer you can always give to any question that catches you off guard.

Ready? Here it is: "I'm not sure. That's a good question. Let me get back to you on that." In business, it's known as the "power stall." But in mentoring it has nothing to do with jockeying for power. It has to do with sincerely wanting to help your mentorees. And they will respect you for it. Besides, nobody really likes a "know-it-all."

So we dedicate this chapter to helping you find answers when you need them and, more importantly, helping you steer clear of answers given in response to questions nobody asked. In other words, we want to remind you to keep advice to a minimum.

WHERE TO FIND THE ANSWERS YOU'RE LOOKING FOR

When a mentoree couple asks a question, the first challenge of every mentor couple is to determine whether or not the mentorees really want an answer. For example, your mentorees might say, "How do you know when you need professional help?" Pretty straightforward, huh? You need to answer it, right? Well, what if the person asking the question quickly followed up with this: "Because I wonder if some couples never get the help they really need. I mean, think of all the pain that could be avoided if they talked to a counselor."

Do you really need to answer this question now? Of course not. The person asking it is simply using it as a springboard to make her point. She's not sincerely interested in knowing when to seek professional help. She's just letting you know she believes in marriage counseling.

Bottom line, every question a mentoree might ask doesn't require an answer. On the other hand, there are those times when you know you're expected to rattle off an informative reply. Say your mentoree asks: "What am I supposed to do when we are having a fight and she leaves the room?" Period. Or more accurately, question mark! What do you say? Neither mentoree is following up. They are looking to you for an answer. Of course, you may have a good answer. In fact, you probably do. You may rely on your own experience to shed some light. But if you are stuck, if

Knowledge is of two kinds. We know a subject ourselves, or we know where we can find information upon it.
SAMUEL JOHNSON

you're not sure exactly what to say, it's time to rely on ol' faithful: "I'm not sure. That's a good question. Let me get back to you on that."

The conversation continues but you make a note to yourself to find them some information that will help. Where do you turn? The Internet? Sure. Any number of websites are possibilities. One of our favorites is www.troubledwith.com.

In addition to the Internet, of course, books can be helpful. Maybe you have a few marriage books on your shelf already. You probably have your favorites that may help on some issues. If you are looking for a book to steer you to specific answers quickly, we humbly suggest a book we wrote

Can You Answer a Question with a Question?
Before We Tell You, What Do You Think?

Your mentorees will ask you questions for a variety of reasons—so don't make the mistake of assuming that they are asking because they want an answer. Their motive behind the question is what's telling. Consider the possibilities.

- Sometimes your mentorees ask questions because they are looking for ammunition to use against their spouse.
- Sometimes they are avoiding what they already know is the right answer, but just don't want to admit it.
- Sometimes they're "smokescreening" with a question to distract everyone from the real issue they'd rather not face.
- Sometimes they are looking for an ally that understands and supports their position.
- Sometimes they are legitimately looking for help!

An important point to remember here is that we are more likely to own something when we articulate it ourselves. So, when a mentoree asks a question like, "What do you think about ...?" often the most powerful answer is, "Before I give you my perspective, what do you think about it?"

Answering a question with a question can help you understand the context in which the question is being asked. Your mentoree may ask a question like: "Do you guys ever argue about dinner?" Now, they may want to genuinely know, but more than likely they are more interested in telling you why they want to know. So you may want to respond by saying something like, "Of course. Why do you ask?"

Answering a question with a question is a terrific tools for marriage mentors.

for just this purpose. Some of the marriage mentors we have trained personally call it their "security blanket." The actual title is *Questions Couples Ask: Answers to the Top 100 Marital Questions*. Whether it be from our mentoring, our counseling, or our seminars, we have collected the most commonly asked questions on marriage and provided answers to them in an easy-to-follow format. You can learn more about this book at www.RealRelationships.com.

> *Advice is like snow — the softer it falls, the longer it dwells upon, and the deeper it sinks into the mind.*
> SAMUEL TAYLOR COLERIDGE

Another helpful resource for marriage mentors is other couples. When you have a question you're not sure how to answer, one of your best resources might be a pastor, a counselor, or a friend. Or maybe another marriage mentor. In fact, many mentors find it helpful to meet from time to time with other mentors and share ideas for this very reason. Perhaps your church can arrange for these periodic meetings.

Well there you have it. A few considerations for answering whatever questions your mentorees might throw at you. No need to be intimidated. You aren't expected to be a know-it-all. Which brings us to one more topic we feel compelled to address before leaving this chapter: advice giving. It seems for some mentors, it can be a bit overused.

WHY ADVICE CAN TURN SOUR

Too often, advice cuts the heart out of effective mentoring. As we often say, a little advice, like a little garlic, goes a long way. Even when they ask you questions, mentorees often don't want advice. They typically just want to connect. They want you to be real, not necessarily knowledgeable. If you are prone to be a trigger-happy advice giver, take a little advice from us and tone it down. Why? Here are a few good reasons:

Advice is often self-centered.

When we dole out advice not cushioned by active listening, what we think is helpful is usually ineffective and often self-serving. It hurts to see another couple struggle, but by doing our part—bestowing advice—we feel better. The driving motive behind eager advice often is a desire to feel good about ourselves.

Advice can make a couple feel worse.

Offering advice can set a couple up to feel worse because they cannot or are not ready to follow through on it. This can instill terrible pangs of guilt. The advice that Job's friends gave him in his time of affliction, for example, only served to make Job more miserable. The only way a mentor can know when and if a couple is ready for advice is through persistent and sensitive listening.

Advice can be threatening.

Sometimes giving advice can call another person's beliefs and attitudes into question. When we do this, it is typically because we're insecure about our own personal beliefs and values, and that's uncomfortable. So, we reason, if we convert a couple to our way of thinking, it would not only relieve our discomfort, it would be further proof of the validity of our beliefs — and cast us into the role of an all-knowing mentor, to boot.

Advice can be boring.

Being forced to sit through an unrewarding or even irritating monologue causes people to turn off the one-way conversation and think

> *Reckless words pierce like a sword, but the tongue of the wise brings healing.*
> PROVERBS 12:18

about something else. Bored listeners simply suppress their impulse to walk out by taking a mental vacation. Without self-restraint, the bored couple would be like the antsy young child at church who looked up at his mom and said, "Pay the man and let's go home." Advice given without active listening (as discussed in the next chapter) causes boredom. And as Proverbs 18:13 says, answering without listening is a person's folly and shame.

Questions, answers, and more questions. Let's next move to a powerful tool for making conversations even deeper and more real — how you and your spouse tell your stories — in chapter 15.

in chapter 15.

REAL-LIFE EXAMPLE OF *Fielding Any Question They Throw at You*

Lorenzo and Bethany, married twenty-seven years, were eager to become marriage mentors. Their only apprehension was that mentoree couples would ask them questions for which they didn't know the answers.

"Neither of us has even graduated from college," Bethany confides. "We aren't worried about having *all* the answers — we'd just like to have *some* of the answers. I'm afraid our mentorees will see right through us and think we're imposters."

After going through mentor training, however, Lorenzo and Bethany's fears were put to rest. "It was comforting to know that we can always reply with 'I'm not sure. That's a good question. Let me get back to you on that,'" said Lorenzo. "Before our training I thought I'd have to read up on everything I could about marriage. Instead, I learned I just need to be myself and, on occasion, help our mentorees find answers to their questions if need be."

And that's exactly what this couple did. In one instance, they had a mentoree couple, newly married, who asked how long they should wait before having children. Lorenzo laughed out loud: "You may be asking the wrong mentors, we had our first baby ten months after being married!" They all laughed. "But let me look into that for you guys and let's see if there is a certain amount of time that's best."

At their next session, Lorenzo and Bethany came with a little more knowledge than they had the time before. "I talked to our pediatrician this week when I took our son in for a checkup and learned that the research shows that couples who wait a few years are usually better prepared to have kids."

"That makes sense," the new husband quickly jumped in, "because that allows your marriage some time to get established."

"And to get your career underway," adds Lorenzo. "After all, if you have a little more money, raising a baby can be a little less stressful."

The young bride also had something to offer: "As you know, I was the one who was eager to start a family, but I actually did some research on the Internet this week and found out that some studies say that couples who wait as much as seven years have the best experience as parents — and as a couple."

It was this interaction, and dozens of others, that make Lorenzo and Bethany feel like they could field any question their mentorees throw at them. "Thank goodness we don't have to be know-it-alls to be good mentors," says Bethany.

CHAPTER 15

TELLING YOUR STORIES

Tell people what you're afraid of,
and you make them your allies.
JAMES D. BERKLEY

Over thirty years ago, a high school journalism teacher and a carload of students heard Grand Ole Opry regular Jerry Clower spin a tale over the radio about coon hunting in Mississippi. And the teacher—Jimmy Neil Smith—had a sudden inspiration: Why not start a storytelling festival?

On a warm October weekend in 1973 in Jonesborough, Tennessee, the first National Storytelling Festival was held. Hay bales and wagons were the stages, and audience and tellers together didn't number more than sixty. It was tiny, but it was a start.

Now acclaimed as one of the Top 100 Events in North America, the festival sparked a renaissance of storytelling across the country. To spearhead that revival, Smith and a few other story lovers founded the National Storytelling Association. The founding organization became the center of an ever-widening movement that continues to gain momentum to this day. Storytelling organizations, festivals, and educational events have popped up all over the world. Teachers, healthcare workers, therapists, corporate executives, librarians, pastors, parents, and others regularly make storytelling a vibrant part of their everyday lives and work.

The story of how this storytelling movement began is an often-told story itself! It has been told in the *Los Angeles Times*, magazines as diverse as *People* and *Smithsonian*, and on and on. Why? No matter the reason, it's a classic example of how a simple story breathes life into information people want to share with each other. As millions of story lovers all over the world already know, there is no substitute for the power, simplicity, and basic truth of a story.

What does this have to do with marriage mentoring? Plenty. One of your primary tools for guiding mentorees is your own story. Or more 151 accurately, your stories — plural. You see, stories stick. They captivate us. It doesn't matter if the story is sad, happy, funny, sentimental, historical, fictitious, mythological, it will drive home a principle more successfully than any other teaching tool. Especially when that story relates to our own life — when we see *ourselves* in the story.

They say I tell a great many stories; I reckon I do, but I have found in the course of a long experience that common people are more easily informed through the medium of a broad illustration than in any other way.

ABRAHAM LINCOLN

So with this in mind, allow us to highlight a few facts about stories and how these facts relate to marriage mentoring. We start with the fact that stories are like glue.

STORIES STICK

Try teaching a solid principle without telling a story and see how quickly it fades. Trust us. We teach for a living. Whenever we encounter one of our university graduates years after being in the classroom, they never say, "I still remember that point you made on a particular theory about such and such." But they are likely to say, "I still remember that day in class when you talked about how your son was born prematurely."

Why would students who graduated seven years ago still remember a story when they've forgotten most of what they read in a textbook? Because stories are like glue. They attach themselves to our lives because we personally identify with the storyteller's feelings or actions or thoughts.

This isn't just conjecture, by the way. Research supports the idea of being able to relate your thoughts and ideas through story. In fact, one recent study revealed that those who use story as a means of relating to others and teaching information engender greater authenticity and self-esteem than those who don't. Storytelling makes others feel good. They feel better about themselves in the process of hearing a story.[1] No wonder stories stick!

STORIES ARE MEANT TO BE SHARED

A Mercedes-Benz TV commercial shows their car colliding with a cement wall during a safety test. Someone then asks the company spokesman why they do not enforce their patent on the Mercedes-Benz energy-absorbing car body, a design evidently copied by other companies because of its success. He replies matter-of-factly, "Because some things in life are too important not to share."

It's true. Whether it's about saving lives through automobile safety or saving marriages through marriage mentoring, some stories are just too important not to share. We mentioned Retrouvaille in chapter 7, "Mentoring Couples in Distress." With a phenomenal success rate in helping couples on the brink of divorce you might think they have an elaborate, sophisticated system of steps in their process. But they don't. Their whole program centers on stories. Couples who have been right where these other couples have been simply tell their stories of being stuck and then starting over. And if you ask any couple who has been helped during one of these weekends—a couple about to file for divorce but who turned it around—they will likely attribute much of it to a real-life story they heard from another couple.

If storytelling can do that for couples in distress, think what it can do for newlyweds or a couple about to have a baby or any of us who can see ourselves in another couple's story. Like we said, stories are meant to be shared. They are one of the greatest tools marriage mentors have.

STORIES REQUIRE VULNERABILITY

One of the books that made a tremendous impact on both of us during our graduate school days was never required reading for any of our classes. But we read it and studied it just the same. *The Wounded Healer* by Henri Nouwen reveals a scintillating truth for anyone in the helping professions: you can't keep your own experiences of life hidden from those you want to help.

"No minister can offer service without a constant and vital acknowledgment of his own experiences," says Nouwen. In other words, to come alongside another person and help them heal and grow, you must be willing to confide your own stories of struggle.

"On the other hand, it would be very easy to misuse the concept of the wounded healer by defending a form of spiritual exhibitionism," Nouwen also says. "A minister who talks in the pulpit about his own personal experiences is of no help to his congregation, for no suffering human being is helped by someone who tells him he has the same problems."[2] Right. Vulnerability is essential but not sufficient. To say "I'm confused (or depressed) too" helps no one. We must be sure to tell stories of hope and healing. Our vulnerability must serve to take our mentorees further down the healing path.

The point is, for your stories to be helpful you must be somewhat vulnerable. Tell all? Of course not. But tell enough about yourselves and your relationship on occasion that your mentorees identify with you and learn from your success as well as the times when you stumbled.

STORIES REQUIRE HUMILITY

Greg Asimakoupoulos, a minister in Naperville, Illinois, tells the story of a wedding where he officiated, but in retrospect wished he hadn't. "I proofread funeral and wedding programs before they are printed at the church," he writes. "On one occasion, the groom printed the programs at a local print shop, and I didn't have an opportunity to proof them."

"While a string quartet played classical music, the wedding guests arrived and were handed a program." Greg looked down at his program. Everything looked fine until his eyes locked on the word signaling where his brief sermon would take place. *Meditation* read *Mediation*. "I wondered how the groom could have been so careless," he complains.

"Making light of the error, I called the congregation's attention to the typo. I suggested that my meditation was intended to give the couple advice that would keep them from ever needing mediation."

But that wasn't the only slip-up that day. Three days later Greg got a call from the county clerk's office saying that he needed to sign a new marriage license for the couple. "I misspelled the groom's last name when I was filling out the document. I had judged the groom's ineptness prematurely. I too made a mistake. Instead of enjoying a leftover slice of wedding cake, I had to eat humble pie."

> *If I only had a little humility, I'd be perfect.*
> TED TURNER

Ever felt like that? Of course. We all have. Every one of us makes mistakes. And it's sometimes our mistakes that make the best stories for the couples we mentor. Why? Because vulnerability begets vulnerability. When your mentorees hear you tell a story of your frailty, they are likely to confide their own imperfections and shortcomings. And this gives you a terrific opportunity to enter their lives at a profound level. This is when marriage mentoring gets real.

If you've ever attended one of our seminars in person you know we don't hesitate to reveal to the audience how we so-called "marriage experts" flub up. The audience typically howls when we confess about having a big fight just before we were to speak at a seminar. They love the story revealing how we each still hold on to the way things were done in our homes growing up — even after more than two decades of marriage. And guess what they want to tell us in the intermissions? You guessed it. They want to tell us about a similar story that happened to them. When you humbly reveal your own foibles, vulnerability almost always begets vulnerability.

Humility, by the way, is at the heart of the gospel. Jesus said there is no salvation without humility (Matthew 18:3–4). Paul presented humility as an elemental aspect of Christian character (Ephesians 4:1–2) and revealed Christ's own humility when he wrote to the church in Philippi: "And being found in appearance as a man, he [Jesus] humbled himself and became obedient to death — even death on a cross!" (Philippians 2:8).

Storytelling Advice

Shane and Aimee Fookes are two of the sharpest marriage mentors we know. And they know the value of telling a story. Shane, however, confesses that he has to work at it. When we asked him what advice he would give to others in the same boat, here's what he said:

Don't simply share facts and data about your experiences, but add richness and texture. Some people naturally do this; others, like me, need to work at it. Here's an example.

STORYTELLING, TAKE 1

One of my most painful experiences when I was a kid happened when I broke my arm after a kid pushed me off a ledge at church onto a concrete walkway. Wow, did that hurt.

STORYTELLING, TAKE 2

Oh man, I vividly remember the day I broke my arm as a kid. Outside an old-time Pentecostal church, as the parents yakked endlessly, we kids entertained ourselves by busily jumping off the tall part of the steps that led up to the sanctuary doors. On this particular bright, sunny day, the queue to jump was long and the toddler set grew restless. When I paused briefly before jumping, the boy behind me impatiently gave me a shove onto the concrete below and introduced me to a threshold of pain only known to those who have broken bones.

How to Tell a Good Story

This brings us to the inevitable question: If stories stick, if they are meant to be shared, if they require vulnerability and humility, then how do you tell a good story?

As a marriage mentor, you tell a good story when you relate to your mentorees something personal about your own marriage relationship.

You tell a good story when you keep in mind that your story is not about you. It's about your mentorees. If you love telling stories, great! Just make sure your mentorees love it as much as you do.

You tell a good story when you poke fun at yourselves. Your mentorees will enjoy knowing that you're not perfect.

While some stories are purely for entertainment, most of your stories should convey a point. You don't want your mentorees to walk away saying, "What was that about?" but rather, "That story reminds me of us; maybe we should do the same thing." Or "That story was powerful; I want to be sure we don't make the same mistake."

You tell a good story when you tell them sparingly. While storytelling is essential to marriage mentoring, it's not the goal. Your meetings with your mentorees are not about coming in with a program or routine and stepping on stage. You tell a good story when your stories are spontaneous and relevant to what you are discussing.

You tell a good story when you both tell a story together, freely interrupting each other to be sure your mentorees see both sides.

You tell a good story when you also provide space and a listening ear to hear your mentorees' stories.

We've saved one of the most precious "skills" for near the end of this section on mentoring tools, because prayer is not really a skill. In the next chapter we'll look at the role that our conversation with God can have in our relationships with our mentorees.

Telling Your Stories

Robert and Claire, marriage mentors to couples wanting to move from good to great, never felt like expert storytellers but they are better than they think. Why? To begin with, after twenty-eight years of marriage they have plenty of stories! But more importantly, they are willing to be vulnerable. Each of them is comfortable in their own skin and willing to let others in on their lives. They don't mind "laying it out" in an honest fashion to make a memorable point.

The suitcase is a good example. "Oh yes," says Claire, "the suitcase!" They can both launch into a now-humorous story about how after a trip they made many years ago they had a little silent spat about who was taking responsibility for putting away the suitcase afterward. It was silent because each of them was ignoring it. The piece of luggage sat just inside the kitchen from the door leading from the garage. And it sat. Neither one of them was claiming it and they both wanted the other to put it away. It was a classic power struggle. To hear them tell the story is a treat. They will have you rolling. But also identifying. After all, what couple hasn't experienced a power struggle? We may not all feel comfortable being vulnerable about it (like Robert and Claire) but we've all experienced it.

Another thing that makes this couple especially good at telling stories is how they keep the point of the story off themselves. In other words, they don't tell a story about themselves to say "look at us." They have an easy way of bringing their attention quickly back to their mentorees. And more often than not, their mentorees reciprocate with a story about themselves that brings up a teachable moment. For example, after telling a story about how they once had routine fights about their differing time schedules (Robert typically more on schedule than Claire), their mentorees revealed that this was one of their toughest struggles, creating an uneasy tension whenever they head out to church, a movie, dinner with friends, or anywhere that has a scheduled starting time. After twelve years of marriage, their mentorees were embarrassed to even reveal this information but once Robert and Claire shared their story, the mentorees immediately felt safe in sharing as well. And with this knowledge, Robert and Claire were able to explore practical ways of making these times less stressful.

That's the result of telling good stories as a mentoring couple. Robert and Claire never lack for having their mentorees open up because they never hesitate to openly share their own stories.

CHAPTER 16

PRAYING TOGETHER

God does nothing but in answer to prayer.
JOHN WESLEY

A young couple decided to start their honeymoon by kneeling beside their bed to pray. But the bride was more than surprised when she heard her new husband's prayer: "For what we are about to receive may the Lord make us truly thankful."

As strange as it may sound, there is a strong link in marriage between prayer and sex. For one thing, prayer is a more powerful predictor of marital satisfaction than frequency of sexual intimacy. But, get this. Married couples who pray together are 90 percent more likely to report higher satisfaction with their sex life than couples who do not pray together.

Okay. Now that we have your attention on the subject of prayer, let's explore its relevance not only to marriage, but specifically to marriage mentoring.

One of the questions we are often asked when meeting with marriage mentor groups around the country is: Should we pray with our mentorees? Our answer is simple: Of course! Prayer changes people. "Prayer—secret, fervent, believing prayer—lies at the root of all personal godliness," wrote William Carey. It is in prayer that we begin to think God's thoughts and desire the things he desires (see Romans 8:26–27). When we pray, God slowly and graciously reveals to us how our lives can be different. Through prayer we start to see our relationships—especially our marriages—from his point of view.

The great giants of the faith viewed prayer as the main source of direction in their lives. Martin Luther declared, "I have so much business I cannot get on without spending three hours daily in prayer." John Wesley said, "God does nothing but in answer to prayer," and he backed up his conviction by praying two hours each day. The words of Mark—"Very early in the morning, while it was still dark, Jesus got up, left the house 159 and went off to a solitary place, where he prayed"—stands as a revealing commentary on the lifestyle of the Son of God himself (Mark 1:35).

Fortunately, you don't have to be a "giant in the faith" to pray. In fact, you may feel like a beginner just learning to pray (even the disciples, in Luke 11:1, implored Jesus, "Lord, teach us to pray"). But as long as you are spending time in prayer—on your own, with your spouse, or with your mentorees—you can be assured that God will make himself present.

For this reason, we feel compelled to include a chapter on prayer because it's a powerful tool in the hands of any marriage mentor. We'll consider prayer from three angles as it relates to the task of marriage mentoring: first, how to effectively pray *with* your mentorees; second, ways to encourage your mentorees to pray as a couple *on their own*; and third, how to pray for your mentoree couple *when you are not with them*.

PRAYING WITH YOUR MENTOREES

Few couples we have mentored were more devout than Tom and Kathleen. They attended church regularly. Kathleen sang in the choir, Tom taught junior high Sunday school. Kathleen was in a women's Bible study, Tom was in a men's accountability group. Everyone in their church looked to Tom and Kathleen as dedicated and vibrant spiritual leaders. But when we first met them, their five-year-old marriage was floundering. They told us their story, one we had heard many times. They were over-involved with everything but their marriage and, as a result, had "fallen out of love." Despite all their spiritual fervor, Tom and Kathleen had neglected the soul of their marriage.

At last, one of us gently probed, "When was the last time the two of you prayed together?" Tom and Kathleen looked at each other and the answer was obvious: it had been a long, long time.

> *More things are wrought by prayer than this world dreams of.*
>
> ALFRED LORD TENNYSON

We gave Tom and Kathleen a simple assignment, an experiment really. For the next week they were to pray briefly together at some point in their day, even if it was only for a minute or simply to recite the Lord's Prayer (see Matthew 6:9–13).

Tom and Kathleen agreed to do this and we then spent a few moments right there in our mentoring session praying for them. We didn't want to put pressure on them to pray with us, so we just uttered a heartfelt prayer for them, asking that God would help them follow through on the assignment. We also told them that we would commit to pray for them each day that week as they were praying together.

Six days later we received a call. "This is Kathleen. I know this sounds crazy, but our relationship has done an about-face." She told us how spending a moment together in prayer was rejuvenating their spirits and their marriage.

No amount of being "religious" can make up for the time couples spend in shared prayer. Yet prayer can be a challenge for even the most

> *Do not pray for tasks equal to your powers. Pray for power equal to your tasks.*
> PHILLIPS BROOKS

devout. That's why praying with your mentorees is important. It's good modeling. It shows your mentorees how they can do this together.

If you want a little specific guidance on how to pray with your mentoree couples, let us tell you what we do. Typically near the end of a mentoring session, we'll ask them if we can pray together. We never make them feel like they have to pray aloud with us but if we pick up that they are open to that we certainly welcome them to do so. Whether they pray aloud or not, we almost always ask them to answer three questions so that we can make our prayers more meaningful. We ask:

- As you review this past week, what are you most thankful for in your partner?
- What's a pressure point the two of you are likely to encounter in your upcoming week?
- What's one positive and concrete action for improving your marriage that you'd like to take this week?

Once they answer these three questions we simply pray with their responses in mind. We give thanks to the Lord for what they are most appreciative of in the previous week. We pray for the pressure points each of them is facing in the upcoming week. And we pray that God would give them the courage and discipline to follow though on the one concrete action they desire to take in the upcoming week.

Of course, we never limit our prayers to just these items but this little list often helps us pray in very specific terms for our mentorees.

ENCOURAGING YOUR MENTOREES TO PRAY TOGETHER

We'll be honest. Praying together is not easy for us. Oh, we pray as a couple before meals, and we pray together when there is a special need or crisis, but we aren't the kind of couple who kneels beside our bed each night. We might be better persons if we did, but we don't. I suppose we could blame our busy and fickle schedules, but the truth is we just haven't made the effort to build a consistent shared prayer time into our lives.

We admire couples who do and we covet the rewards they surely reap. For as Jesus has said, "If two of you on earth agree about anything you ask for, it will be done for you by my Father in heaven. For where two or three come together in my name, there am I with them" (Matthew 18:19–20).

Still, one thing we do every day is pray for each other. Whether together or in separate cities, we remember each other in our daily prayers. We made that commitment on our wedding day and Leslie had the reference of Philippians 1:3–11 engraved inside my wedding band. It's a prayer that begins with these words: "I thank my God every time I remember you … I always pray with joy because of your partnership in the gospel from the first day until now."

Sometimes one of us will say to the other, "I'll be praying for you today," but most of the time there is just a quiet assurance that our partner is lifting us up with prayers.

So what's our point? Every couple finds their own way to pray in marriage. What works for you may not work for your mentorees and vice versa. However, no Bible-believing person can ignore the fact that every couple is better off when they pray. So, when the time is right, don't ignore this point in your mentoring. Be real. Be genuine. Be vulnerable. Be gentle.

> *Prayer isn't about impressing anyone, it's about communicating what's on your heart.*
> SHANE FOOKES

But, eventually, it's a good subject for conversation. Talk about how the two of you pray in your own marriage in a way that will encourage your mentorees to find their own style of prayer together.

You may even want to remind them what sociologist Andrew Greeley found when he surveyed married people. He discovered that the most powerful correlate of marital happiness is praying together. Couples who frequently pray together are twice as likely as those who pray less often to describe their marriages as being highly romantic. That's reason enough to broach the subject of prayer with your mentorees.

PRAYING FOR YOUR MENTOREES

Søren Kierkegaard once observed: "A man prayed, and at first he thought that prayer was talking. But he became more and more quiet until in the end he realized that prayer is listening." Listening to God is the necessary prelude to intercession. We must hear the still, small voice of God before we pray into the life of our mentorees. This is the starting place when it comes to praying for them.

Of course, the same three questions we pose to our mentorees about their past week and the week ahead often direct our prayers for them between meetings. We pray that God will help them through their pressure points and give them strength to practice this week what they set out to, and so on. But, above all, we take time to listen to what God is prompting us to pray for. We meditate on how he is guiding us with our mentorees.

> *Grant that I may not pray alone with the mouth; help me that I may pray from the depths of my heart.*
> MARTIN LUTHER

In times of meditation, Richard Foster points out, there may come a rise in the heart, a compulsion of compassion to intercede. We are told that Jesus was moved with compassion for people (see Matthew 9:36). This compassion is one of the clearest indications that you are being called to prayer for your mentorees. After all, when you genuinely mentor a couple, you desire for them far more than is within your power to give, and that will cause you to pray.

Just two more skills to cover and you'll be well on your way to being star marriage mentors! Let's look in the next chapter at how you can ensure that you stay sharp and renewed.

REAL-LIFE EXAMPLE OF *Praying Together*

Ted and Gwen, married more than two decades, love being marriage mentors. They are the first to tell you that the "boomerang effect" is evidenced in their lives; in other words, they are quick to recognize what mentoring does for their own marriage.

"The only thing that has been a bit of a struggle in our years of mentoring has concerned the issue of prayer," says Ted. "Gwen is a prayer warrior. She loves to pray. And I love it that she loves to pray. It's just that I don't pray like she does."

Ted goes on to say that prayer, for him, has traditionally been a very private and personal matter. Not that he doesn't pray aloud at the dinner table and so on, but he doesn't naturally pray with other people the way Gwen does.

"I can't help myself," says Gwen. "I find such comfort and strength in prayer and I know it makes such a difference in people's lives. That's why I like to pray for the couples we mentor. If they are struggling financially, I pray that they will make wise money decisions and so forth."

Nearly every day Gwen prays for the couples they are working with. And at the close of their mentoring sessions, she can't imagine forgoing prayer together. This sometimes puts Ted on the spot. It makes him feel uneasy. At least it used to. These days, he often initiates a prayer with his mentorees, asking them how he and Gwen can pray for them in the coming days.

"I used to think I had to pray like a pastor or that my prayers needed to be long and eloquent," he says. "But no more. Today, I simply say a brief prayer with our mentorees and I also let them know that both Gwen and I will be praying for them. I think it brings them a lot of comfort."

Because mentorees know they are being prayed for throughout any given week, it's not unusual for Ted and Gwen to receive an email from them requesting prayer for a specific concern or need. And, by the way, Ted and Gwen also find that many of their mentorees pray for them as well.

CHAPTER 17

STAYING SHARP
AND REFRESHED

The doorstep to the temple of wisdom is a knowledge
of our own ignorance.
Charles Haddon Spurgeon

Recently we spoke to a large group of soldiers at Fort Lewis, just south of
Tacoma, Washington, giving a talk on "military marriages" with the help
of several chaplains. One of the officials escorting us around the base prior
to our talk pointed out a group of men who were being trained to become
part of an elite group of soldiers that would operate very technical equip-
ment in specially designed tanks.

"Not all of them will make it," he confided to us.

"Why's that?" Les asked.

"Because upgrading your training and continually doing maintenance
drills—often on your own time—is never an urgent need."

His answer startled us. "What do you mean?"

"All of these men know that what they are learning and practicing is
important but other tasks, more urgent jobs, keep many of them from getting to it. And those that don't show initiative and make this continual
training a priority will fail."

"That's true of nearly anything worthwhile in life," Les added.

"You've got that right," said the captain.

Important but not urgent. This phrase (unfortunately so) describes the
marriage mentoring skill of learning all you can. And it is perfectly illus-
trated by Stephen Covey in his popular book *The Seven Habits of Highly
Effective People.* He calls it "sharpening the saw," an idea best described by
Covey's own word-picture:

> Suppose you were to come upon someone in the woods working feverishly
> to saw down a tree.

165

"What are you doing?" you ask.

"Can't you see?" comes the impatient reply. "I'm sawing down this tree."

"You look exhausted!" you exclaim. "How long have you been at it?"

"Over five hours," he returns, "and I'm beat! This is hard work."

"Well, why don't you take a break for a few minutes and sharpen that saw?" you inquire. "I'm sure it would go a lot faster."

"I don't have time to sharpen the saw," the man says emphatically. "I'm too busy sawing!"[1]

You get the point. "Sharpening the saw is about renewal. It's about improvement. It's about learning. It's about staying, well, sharp. And it's vital to marriage mentoring. Why? Because your mentoring can only be as good as you are. *You* are the instrument. You and your marriage are the tools being used to help another couple. That's why, in this chapter, we focus on two key components to staying sharp as marriage mentors: (1) self improvement and self renewal, and (2) marriage improvement and marriage renewal. Both of them deserve equal attention from anyone who is serious about marriage mentoring. So let's take a good look at each.

SELF IMPROVEMENT

The ancient dictum of Socrates to "know thyself" is critical to becoming an effective marriage mentor. Self-knowledge allows mentors to identify personal limits and become more objective. It empowers mentors to know what they are doing, why they are doing it, which problems are theirs, and which belong to the couple they are working with. When mentors know themselves, and are comfortable with themselves, they are more at ease in working with others.

How can you become more self-aware? For some, a journal can be a terrific means. Self-awareness increases when you record thoughts, feelings, experiences, stories, dreams, and prayers. Our written expressions are often different from what we might disclose verbally, and they can teach us much about who we are. To be clear, the journaling we are talking about here is to track your own issues and personal growth, not that of your mentorees (though that certainly has its place).

Your self-awareness also can be heightened by asking questions that target important areas of your inner life. To begin with, ask "Do I feel secure?" Mentors who are secure have little need to pass judgment on others, and they are confident enough to allow other couples to develop at their own rates and in their own directions. Insecure mentors, on the other hand, are less accurate in their ability to recall words and feelings expressed by their mentorees. They may even have a tough time following what the couple is saying.

Next, ask yourself, "Do I trust other people?" The mentor who is suspicious and cynical is not likely to relate to mentorees in ways conducive to healthy change and growth. Mistrustful mentors project feelings and ideas onto the couple that do not exist. For example, a mentor who feels angry projects this feeling onto the mentoree and asks, "Why are you so negative today?"

Another question is, "Do I have the courage to confront challenges?" Mentors must have the courage to confront themselves — to examine their true motives, feelings, and limitations. Mentors must also have the courage to confront their mentorees and be willing, at times, to subjugate their own feelings and desires to be liked, respected, and admired in favor of helping their mentorees make progress.

Self-awareness and improvement can also come by asking your spouse and other trusted friends (or even a personal coach) for feedback. We realize that this can be scary, but people who know you well can be invaluable in this area. They may see things in you that you might never see on your own.

There's one more powerful means toward self improvement that we feel compelled to note — prayer and meditation. In fact, writing in *Discipleship Journal*, William Farley gives a graphic depiction of how this works:

> The Lord arrested me with Isaiah 66:2: "This is the one I esteem: he who is humble and contrite in spirit, and trembles at my word." I wanted a deeper relationship with God, and I felt impressed that this verse had something to do with it. But I didn't understand the connection between humility and trembling before God's Word. So I prayed, "Lord, please make this verse real to me."
>
> Five days later my wife and I were driving down the Oregon coast. While I was meditating on 1 Corinthians 13, another verse caught my attention. "Now I know in part; then I shall know fully, even as I am fully known." I realized that God saw spiritual darkness in me to which I was blind, that he loved me despite this spiritual cancer, and that someday he would let me see it as he saw it. I prayed again, "God, please open my eyes to this evil in my heart."
>
> As we followed Highway 101 south, I sensed a connection between Isaiah 66:2 and 1 Corinthians 13:12. So I prayed a third time: "God, show me the connection between those verses."

A few minutes later my wife began talking about a movie she liked. Irritated by the intrusion of such a trivial topic into my meditation, I condescendingly belittled her opinion. Instantly, three life-changing words knifed into my consciousness. They weren't audible, but they came so suddenly and were so completely non-volitional that I lurched behind the steering wheel.

THERE IT IS!

What was that? I wondered. Then I realized that God had spoken to me. So I asked, "What is it?" An overwhelming sense of the moral ugliness of it—my arrogance and pride—washed over me. For the first time, I saw this sin in God's light.

My next sensation was the profound conviction that God had loved me for 45 years despite this besetting sin he abhorred. For a moment, he let me know myself as he knew me. It was painful to see my pride as God saw it. Yet I was glad for that glimpse. I wept for my sin, and I wept because of God's indescribable love.[2]

SELF RENEWAL

In addition to becoming more self-aware, the effective mentor also takes time for renewal. For many of us, this means replenishing our spirit. It means taking time for what is important, not just what's urgent. To paraphrase C. S. Lewis: "A mentor cannot always be about teaching truth, he must also feed on it."

What are you doing to feed your spirit? How are you letting your soul catch up? How are you taking care of yourself? Because you have the heart of a marriage mentor—you wouldn't be reading this if you didn't—you may be prone to "compassion fatigue." You may be inclined to place everyone's needs before your own. It's an admirable trait, no doubt, but it can be taken too far if you never allow yourself time for renewal.

Much of the world scoffs at the tradition of the siesta in Italy, Spain, and Mexico. Americans in particular smirk at the French practice of closing down in August and Sweden's mandated five-week minimum vacation policy.

Most people in North America (and certain other places around the globe) have never been comfortable with the abstract notion of free time. It is not in our nature to just let time pass. Unstructured time, dead time, downtime, wasted time. It makes us ill at ease. In fact, for some of us, it literally makes us sick.

Consider a typical scenario: The weekend's finally here. You're ready to let down and relax. But you're headachy, tired, or you've got a stiff neck and maybe even coming down with the flu. Researchers at Tilburg University in the Netherlands say it strikes perfectionists or people who carry large workloads and feel very responsible at their job. These people are more apt to suffer from these symptoms, termed "leisure sickness," and they have a tough time making the transition from the daily grind to home life.

> *Knowledge is horizontal.*
> *Wisdom is vertical — it*
> *comes down from above.*
>
> BILLY GRAHAM

The Dutch researcher Vingerhoets began his study after noticing that some of his own weekends and vacations were spent suffering through headaches and other physical ailments. He tried to find out if any studies had been done on the perplexing phenomenon and found none. So Vingerhoets, whose research area is stress and emotions, decided to study the subject himself.

The researcher and his team observed more than a hundred people who were plagued by headaches, muscle pain, fatigue, and nausea over weekends and holidays. Most of the subjects reported suffering from these symptoms in their downtimes for more than ten years.

Other explanations for your leisure sickness, according to the researcher: "You may be more aware of your symptoms in a quiet environment as opposed to the hectic workplace," says Vingerhoets. Or your body could be staving off illness until you can slow down.[3]

The solution? For some it's as simple as sleep. Did you get your nightly requirement this week?

At the end of many entries in his famous diaries depicting the early Restoration period in England, Samuel Pepys signed off with an endearing phrase: "And so to bed." For Pepys, those four little words marked the end of another day in seventeenth-century London. In today's world, the phrase could serve as a clever rallying cry for a fledgling movement that wants to encourage people to catch more z's.

Once, new parents constituted the primary group of sleep-deprived adults. Now two-thirds of Americans don't get eight hours of sleep every night, according to the National Sleep Foundation. The result, the group says, is a nation of sleepyheads.

If you're like most people, you need more sleep. It may be key to your personal renewal. Another key, however, is found in recreation.

Consider the facts. A survey by Management Recruiters International Inc., the world's largest search and recruitment organization, shows that a mind-boggling 82 percent of our vacations include bringing work with us. Seems these days we're more inclined to have a "working vacation." Can you believe it? We're even stuffing our time to play with work by phoning the office and emailing colleagues. Thirteen percent of us admit to shortening our vacations once we are on them because of work.[4]

And it's not just vacations that are getting bamboozled by work. Seems our weekends are also at risk. Less than a quarter of people today associate weekends with having fun. A poll of more than a thousand respondees reveals that one in seven women find the weekend is a time when depression sets in about the week ahead.[5]

We could go on. The research on how most of us are running ourselves ragged is staggering. The bottom line is that if we are to stay sharp as marriage mentors, we have to give ourselves time to renew our spirit.

Of course, we also need to give attention not only to ourselves but to our marriage.

Marriage Improvement

Rodney Clapp describes an intriguing thought in a *Marriage Partnership* article: "Sometimes I look at Sandy sleeping, unaware of me, vulnerable as a child," he writes. "The face of a sleeping woman, of this sleeping woman, is profound. With its soft lines, with its hidden eyes, with its closed lips, it says: 'Eleven years are barely enough to get beneath the skin — let alone to the heart — of the mystery that is a person.' This woman is my wife. But she is also a sweet stranger, beyond the knowing of a lifetime. She surprises me. I am glad for that, I really am, because it renews our marriage."[6]

We know what he means. Do you? Learning about our spouse is a lifelong proposition. The study is never complete. He or she is the ultimate mystery that, even after many years, can surprise us. That's why "marriage improvement" is another key to this mentoring skill.

Chances are that the two of you as marriage mentors are already fairly diligent about improving your marriage. But it never hurts to consider ways for sharpening your marital saw. Allow us to explore just a few ideas.

One of the most common ways to keep your marriage tuned up is through a marriage seminar or workshop. We should know. We conduct marriage seminars many times around the country each year. In fact, on any given Saturday you are likely to find us in a church somewhere talking to several hundred couples who have carved out a precious day of their weekend to get a marriage tune-up. And we never take this task for granted. We always say a special prayer for these couples we have the honor to teach. And more often than not, by the time we fly back to our home city of Seattle, our email box is full of notes from couples expressing gratitude for something specific that seemed to make a difference for them.

That's what a marriage seminar can do. It can give you a "take-away," something practical to do right away that makes a positive difference in your marriage.

> *If your soul has no Sunday,*
> *it becomes an orphan.*
> ALBERT SCHWEITZER

Another tool for improving your marriage, of course, is a good book. Some time ago we were in the home of our friends Jerry and Sharyn Regier for a lovely dinner. "Wow," we said, as we looked at the bookcase in their family room, "you two read a lot of marriage books." Jerry went on to tell us that they have long been intentional about studying marriage and that some of their best discussions as a couple stem from a marriage book they are reading together. It's true for most couples: reading a marriage book from time to time keeps you sharp.

Here's another thought: being mentored. That's right. We know you are mentoring other couples, but what about being mentored yourselves? We've been married more than two decades but we still have a marriage mentor — in fact, we always have. We're not coping with a crisis. We're not particularly journeying through a tough patch. But we still feel the need for an objective couple in our lives who will speak truth. This may not be practical for you, but it's been a gift to us and it continues to build our marriage. It's something worth considering.

MARRIAGE RENEWAL

In addition to improving your marriage, every marriage mentor couple needs to be intentional about renewing their marriage. And one of the most effective ways to renew the soul of your marriage is to "remember the Sabbath and keep it holy." God first commands the Sabbath to the Israelites in Exodus, with the initial revelation of the Ten Commandments, and then again in Deuteronomy. Perhaps because of this, it's easy to look at the Jewish Sabbath as a long list of thou shalt nots: don't turn on lights; don't drive; don't cook, don't plan for the week ahead, and so on. What all this boils down to (and boiling is another thing you cannot do on Shabbat) is, do not create. For one of the things the Sabbath reprises is God's rest after he finished creating. The point being that if God rested, we can too. As

Moishe Konigsberg says, "When we don't operate machines, or pick flowers, or pluck fish from the sea ... when we cease interfering in the world we are acknowledging that it is God's world."

Are we suggesting that Christians embrace the strict regulations of the Orthodox Jewish Sabbath? Nope. The New Testament unambiguously inaugurates a new understanding of Shabbat.[7] In his epistles, Paul makes clear that the Sabbath, like other external signs of piety, is insufficient for salvation.[8] But there is something in the Jewish Sabbath that is absent from most Christian Sundays: a true cessation from the rhythms of work and world, a time wholly set apart. Sunday is not meant to be just an add-on to our week. Sunday is our holy day of rest—"set apart" from the other days. When we fail to live a Sabbath truly distinct from weekly time, we are missing out on one of the greatest means God has given us to find rest—rest in him.[9]

> *Time given to inner renewal is never wasted. God is not in a hurry.*
> HENRI J. NOUWEN

So we ask: How are you keeping the Sabbath? Are you refraining from work, mowing lawns, balancing checkbooks? If so, good for you. If not, you're more like us. By Sunday evening in our house you can feel the workweek creeping in. But we're doing our best to set this day apart and keep it holy. We do more than merely attend church and eat a leisurely brunch. We take a walk. We talk. We read. It's not much, but it has more to do with what we don't do than what we do. We don't go shopping. We don't churn out email or return calls. We don't lean on the television without intention. Like we said, it's not much, and it's not always consistent, but we're doing our best to set Sunday apart from the other days in our week in an attempt to remember our Creator, replenish our souls, and renew our spirits.

In his book *The Road to Daybreak*, Henri Nouwen writes, "I feel a tension within me. I have only a limited number of years left.... Why not use them well? Time given to inner renewal is never wasted. God is not in a hurry." Whenever we find ourselves feeling as though we're not being productive, when we are tempted to think that our Sabbath is stealing time from what we could be doing to get ahead, we try to remember what Nouwen said. Inner renewal is never wasted.

Well, there you have it. This skill of learning all you can has little to do with your mentorees and everything to do with you. And, at certain junctures in your mentoring efforts, this skill may be one of the most important you ever master.

Our last skill is discussed in the next chapter—being yourself. Should be easy, no?

REAL-LIFE EXAMPLE OF *Staying Sharp and Refreshed*

Kevin and Valerie, married thirty-six years, will tell you straight-up that one of the fringe benefits of mentoring other couples is what it will do for your own marriage. Something almost mystical takes place in your relationship when you are working together to help others.

"It's not just the act of helping others that is beneficial," says Valerie, "it's that marriage mentoring keeps us sharp. It forces us to stay at the top of our game." She goes on to say how both she and Kevin believe that you can only take another couple as far as you have traveled yourselves—"that's one of the reasons we are motivated to sharpen our marriage saw."

How do they do this? For starters, they have a consistent "date night" almost every week. This is a time where they enjoy a leisurely dinner with no cell phones or other intrusions. It's their time to recharge and they diligently protect it. Recently, they've even used this time over dinner to talk about what they are learning when it comes to marriage. Both of them enjoy reading and they typically each have some type of book related to marriage on their nightstand.

"We've made it a little game," says Valerie, "by simply asking, 'What do you know about marriage right now that I don't?'" The point is that they try to educate one another with anything they may have learned in recent days. "There's no pressure," says Kevin. "Sometimes my answer is 'nothing,' but the question almost always generates a good conversation about marriage."

Another thing this couple does is to host a quarterly gathering of other marriage mentors in their church. Sometimes they meet at their home, sometimes at the church, and sometimes at a restaurant. Wherever they meet, they simply talk about their experiences. "This always encourages us," says Valerie. "We kind of let our hair down, share some funny stories, and learn what we can from each other."

Kevin and Valerie also attend a marriage seminar from time to time. They pay attention to news stories that are marriage related, and they receive a couple of email newsletters that help them keep their marriage saw sharp.

CHAPTER 18

BEING YOURSELF AND GOING WITH THE FLOW

You cannot play the piano well
unless you are singing within you.
ARTHUR RUBENSTEIN

"Some time ago some wonderful people in our church gave Anna, my wife, and me a dinner certificate to a nice restaurant for $100," writes Wayne Cordeiro, pastor of New Hope Christian Fellowship O'ahu in Honolulu, Hawaii. "We thought, *Wow, a hundred bucks. Let's go for it.* We found a free evening. We dressed up. I took a bath, used deodorant and cologne—the whole thing. I even washed and waxed my car, because we wanted to take it through the valet, and I didn't want my Ford Pinto to look bad. The night came, and we were excited."

He tells how they went to a ritzy restaurant where they were seated at a candlelit table overlooking a lagoon adjacent to a moonlit bay. "Oh, it was nice. And we thought, for a hundred bucks for just the two of us, we could eat high on the hog. So we ordered the most expensive thing there. It was wonderful."

When the bill came, Wayne said, "Honey, why don't you give me the certificate."

"I don't have the certificate. I thought you brought it," said Anna.

"You have to have it," replied Wayne. "You're supposed to have it. You're the wife!"

When it was obvious that neither of them brought the certificate, Wayne made a startling realization: "We look rich, we act rich, we even smell rich. But if we don't have that certificate, it invalidates everything."[1]

And so it does. The lesson applies to marriage mentoring as well. You can look like you're a great marriage mentor—say the right things, listen attentively, ask meaningful questions, pray together, and all the rest, but if   175 you aren't being authentic, it invalidates every mentoring effort. Mentoring without a real relationship is meaningless.

Essential to being effective as a marriage mentor couple is learning to be yourselves in the process. That means being true to you, not trying to be someone or something you are not.

Every once in a while as we train other mentors, we see a couple who comes off as rather formal, presenting a front that they think makes them seem competent. They don't fess up to any struggles, as if they have it all together and always have, and appear to have an agenda that barely considers their mentorees. They seem, in a word, scripted. What they don't know is that their mentorees will never buy it. Why? Because as we've said before, each of us has a built-in radar detector for phoniness — especially when it comes to a couple we are looking up to.

> *None goes his way alone:*
> *All that we send into*
> *the lives of others comes*
> *back into our own.*
> EDWIN MARKHAM

This is a skill that you cannot neglect. You must become comfortable with yourselves as mentors. Not only that, you have to learn to go with the flow, ride the mentoring waves with your mentorees by allowing them to set the pace and guide the direction. If this doesn't make sense, it will.

Let's take a closer look at what we are talking about.

BEING YOURSELF

"Real isn't how you are made. It's a thing that happens to you," said the toy horse. "When a child loves you for a long, long time, not just to play with, but really loves you, then you become Real."

This old toy horse in Margery Williams's classic children's story, *The Velveteen Rabbit*, squarely identifies the result of a relationship that is loving: you become real. Authentic. You become comfortable in your own skin. And this is essential to effective marriage mentoring.

Being yourself separates the genuine marriage mentor from the one who merely wants to be *seen* as a marriage mentor. It allows no room for imitation or posing. It's not about "phoning it in." And it never simply goes through the motions.

When you are being yourself as a mentor your head and heart work in harmony. You are the same person at home as you are with your mentorees. You're not putting on a show. You are genuine.

Authenticity is all about *being* rather than *doing*. When you focus on being genuinely loving, for example, the actions naturally follow. They are not contrived. There's no pretense. You don't wonder what you should do. Your doing flows naturally from your being.

Consider this statement: "You're the first person I have ever been completely honest with." We've heard that statement from mentorees hundreds of times. Every long-term mentor has. But it was Sidney Jourard who made sense of this in his in-depth book *The Transparent Self.* Puzzled with why people often are more honest and authentic with someone they don't know nearly as well as family or friends, after much study he concluded that each of us has a natural, built-in desire to be known, but out of fear we stifle our vulnerability with the significant people in our lives. We're afraid of being seen as too emotional or not emotional enough, as too assertive or not assertive enough.[2] We're afraid of rejection.

The result? We wear masks. We—both mentors and mentorees—put up our guard. In Margery Williams's story, the toy rabbit didn't know real rabbits existed. He thought they were all stuffed with sawdust like himself. "And he understood that sawdust was quite out-of-date and should never be mentioned in modern circles." The rabbit kept authenticity at bay through his fear of being found out. He never wanted to risk vulnerability.

But we are never authentic until we admit our frustrations, acknowledge our weaknesses, and disclose our insecurities. We are never real until we open our wounded hearts.

> *Goodness consists not in the outward things we do but in the inward things we are.*
> EDWIN HUBBEL CHAPIN

Everyone's heart has been wounded. But most people would rather protect their wounds than divulge them. Authentic marriage mentors, however, make personal wounds available to others when needed.

No one has written more sensitively on the gift of vulnerability than Henri Nouwen (whom we noted in an earlier chapter), in his book *The Wounded Healer.* He points out that "making one's own wounds a source of healing does not call for a sharing of superficial personal pains but for a constant willingness to see one's own pain and suffering as rising from the depth of the human condition."[3]

Authentic marriage mentors are honest about their imperfections, problems, inadequacies, and pain. They do not try to disown their failings or ignore their weaknesses. Instead, they use them to propel themselves forward and in the process build a positive relationship with their mentorees. Does this mean you go out of your way to divulge any and every foible to your mentoree couple? Of course not.

Think of it this way. If four people had to push a car in need of gas across a street, what would be the best way for them to push? Obviously, all four of them pushing together in the same direction would maximize their likelihood of reaching the common goal. When they align their efforts, they multiply their power and optimize their efficiency.

Now imagine that this car represents your personality. And what you think, feel, say, and do are the four people trying to get the car across the street. In order for you to reach your highest goals, these four separate parts of you must work in alignment, all headed in the same direction. *Together.*

One of the surest signs of being genuine, being yourself, is when you no longer ask, "What should I be feeling?" but instead, "What *am* I feeling?" You rely on an internal gyroscope that keeps your psychological bearings steady instead of trying to tiptoe around, guessing what you think others (including your spouse or your mentorees) want you to be. You are being true to you and your mentorees will respect you for it.

Going with the Flow

I (Les) grew up in Boston and whenever we return to that great city I always marvel at the layout of the roads. There appears to be no recognizable city planning in Boston, unlike other cities whose streets and avenues are well-organized. Why is this? Because the roads in Boston were actually formed by cows, not people.

It's true. In the early days, paths were forged by cows moving through the topography and they tended to move where it was easiest. When a cow saw a hill ahead, she did not say to herself "Aha! A hill! I must navigate around it." Rather, she put one foot in front of another, taking whatever step was easiest at the moment. In other words, what determined her behavior was the structure of the land. As more cows followed suit, the path became more recognizable and eventually these cow paths became the city's roads.

This same approach is taken on many college campuses. Before concrete is poured for sidewalks, some campus planners leave a new area of construction surrounded by raw ground to see where the natural flow of traffic will develop and then they lay the sidewalks accordingly.

Once a structure exists, energy moves through the structure by the path of least resistance. In other words, energy moves where it is easiest for it to go. This is true not only for cows or college students but for marriage mentors as well.

Once you get a handle on being yourself with your mentorees, your next task in becoming effective as a mentor is to go with the flow. Just as water in a river flows following the path of least resistance, so does the effective marriage mentor. What does this mean? It means that your job is to discover, as much as it is to create.

This is key. While you will certainly want to create a structure of some kind in which to do your work as a mentor, you do not want your structure to inhibit the work of mentoring or to hamper "happy accidents," those occasions where something wonderful happens even though it wasn't part of your plan.

Just as some well-intentioned mentors make the mistake of trying to play the role of a marriage mentor rather than being themselves, some also try to impose a structure on the mentoring process that doesn't allow for the natural emergence of relationships along the way. They major on creating rather than discovering. In short, they don't "go with the flow."

> *When we get inspired and motivated, it is by real people, the ones with a good head on their shoulders, of course, but always with a heart.*
>
> DAVID STODDARD

So how can you ensure that you go with the flow? By learning from your mentorees as they learn from you. Learn their learning style, for example. While you may be linear, wanting to go from one point to the next, they may be more spontaneous, hopping around from point to point and then back again. Going with the flow means you are sensitive to this.

It also means that you learn about their interests and relate various lessons to activities they can relate to. If they enjoy backpacking, for example, you may be able to use backpacking as an analogy that will more effectively drive home a point for them.

Study their maturity level. If you are feeling a bit impatient with your mentorees for not understanding or practicing something you suggest, it may have more to do with maturity level than with willingness.

You get the idea. The point is that the more you learn about them the more you will be able to go with the flow. And, by the way, this may require letting go of various expectations as well. You may need to let go of a personal agenda, for example. Perhaps you expect your mentorees to have a date night or balance their budget or practice a particular exercise just like you do. And if they don't, then what? If you go with the flow, you'll need to let it go. The goal is to drop your personal agenda. Recognize that they may be quite different from you and they may be developing their own style of doing things.

One more thing. Going with the flow may require you to let go of immediate results. This can be tough. After all, you are invested in this couple. You want to see positive change. But just because you don't see changes taking place on your time schedule doesn't mean you are not making progress. Every couple incorporates new habits and makes changes on their own timeline. Let go of your expectation for immediate results and you'll be that much closer to going with the flow.

REAL LIFE EXAMPLE OF *Being Yourself and Going with the Flow*

Jim and Karen have been married more than forty years. They are both comfortable in their own skin and it shows. They are genuine. They are the real deal. They don't put on airs or pretend to be something they aren't. And it's their ability to be themselves that makes them so winsome and effective as marriage mentors.

"If we can't be true to who we are," says Jim, "we'd hang it up as marriage mentors. Why? Because mentorees can spot phoniness a mile away." And he's right.

How do Jim and Karen do this? One way is by being aware of their own feelings as they interact with mentorees. When their mentorees describe a conflict that makes Jim and Karen wince, they say so. "Boy, as you describe this interaction, I feel my stomach turning into a knot—do you guys feel that same way?" When they watch a mentoree couple interact and the husband seems to keep stepping over his wife's words, Jim might comment: "I do the same thing, don't I, Karen?"

They're not hiding anything. They're not trying to be perfect. Jim and Karen are just true to themselves. On top of that they "go with the flow." They are comfortable letting their mentorees steer the ship from time to time. "I used to be very structured and regimented, not only at work, but in my relationships," Jim confesses.

"I can vouch for that," laughs Karen.

"It's true. I admit it," Jim continues. "I cringe at how I used to compulsively demand order and logic in our relationship. But as I've grown, I've mellowed in this area."

"He's far more easygoing," says Karen, "and so am I. This is certainly a benefit when it comes to marriage mentoring. In our younger days we probably would have needed more structure and order—and Jim would have kept us on task!"

"These days, however, we kind of go where the conversational current takes us," says Jim. "If our mentorees say they want to focus on in-law issues but we seem to end up talking more about how to juggle marriage and work, that's okay. In fact, they know better than we do, most of the time, what they need to explore with us."

A FINAL THOUGHT

Aoccdrnig to rsecaerh at Cmabrigde Uinervtisy, it deosn't mttaer in waht oredr the ltteers in a wrod are, the olny iprmoatnt tihng is taht the frist and lsat ltteer be at the rghit pclae. The rset can be a toatl mses and you can sitll raed it wouthit porbelm. Tihs is bcuseae the huamn mnid deos not raed ervey lteter by istlef, but the wrod as a wlohe.

Okay, before you fire off an email to the publisher about the inexcusable lack of proofreading for typos on this page, we want to be sure you read through the entire paragraph so you get our point. That point being that even with a lot of errors you can still mentor very effectively. You may make some mistakes along the way. Correction. You *will* make some mistakes as you mentor. We all do. But if you bring a genuine heart into this process and invest yourself in another couple's life, you can't fail. Any mistakes you make will be lost in the overwhelming message of support and love you are giving to the couple you mentor.

So as you mentor, never forget the words of Jesus when he said to his disciples:

> "The harvest is plentiful but the workers are few.
> Ask the Lord of the harvest, therefore,
> to send out workers into his harvest field."
> MATTHEW 9:37-38

We wish you every success as you enter the harvest field of marriage mentoring.

APPENDIXES *for*
MARRIAGE
MENTORS

Common Subjects to Explore with Your Marriage Mentorees

As you approach your sessions with a new mentoree couple—whether they fall on the preparing side of the triangle, the maximizing side, or the repairing side—you'll want to think beforehand about what subjects you'd like to explore together. As we've said before, each couple is unique and will have their own set of burning issues (either above or below the surface) to delve into. But it's also good for you to think in advance about potential topics, for in discussing the possibilities with your mentorees, you may bring up an area that they might not readily think of otherwise.

We've covered all of these topics in part 2 of this book, but we thought it would be valuable for you to have them all in one place as well.

TOPICS FOR PREPARING: MENTORING ENGAGED AND NEWLYWED COUPLES

- Establishing marital roles
- Managing conflict
- Handling money
- Enjoying physical intimacy
- Dealing with in-laws
- Celebrating holidays and creating family traditions
- Developing the honeymoon habit

TOPICS FOR MAXIMIZING: MENTORING COUPLES FROM GOOD TO GREAT

- Moving from plodding to purpose
- The need for love talk (communication)
- Moving from selfishness to service
- Parenting with pleasure
- The role of humor and laughter

TOPICS FOR REPAIRING: MENTORING COUPLES IN DISTRESS

- Battling addictions
- Surviving infidelity
- Coping with infertility
- Dealing with loss

What You Will Find for Marriage Mentors at www.RealRelationships.com

Believing that the sustainability of your marriage mentoring ministry requires more than just a book and DVD kit, we want to continually resource you with materials and contacts that will prove helpful as you get up and running. For this purpose we have developed a website just for you at:

www.RealRelationships.com

Here you will find forms you can download, articles with new information and research, assessment tools, new tips for mentors, a place to ask questions, announcements about conferences related to marriage mentors, and a resource for networking you with other marriage mentors. Don't miss out on all the latest updates—we want to be there for you! And please do get in touch with us and tell us your stories, successes, and challenges. We love hearing from you.

Saving Your Marriage Before It Starts: A Tool for Mentoring Engaged and Newlywed Couples

Saving Your Marriage Before It Starts (SYMBIS), first released in 1995, has been used by more than a half million couples. Every week we are humbled to receive emails and letters from grateful couples who found it helpful. (In 2006 an updated and expanded edition and DVD kit will be published.) If you are not familiar with SYMBIS, let us give you a quick snapshot.

The SYMBIS model centers on seven questions every couple needs to ask before and after they marry:

1. Have you faced the myths of marriage with honesty?
2. Can you identify your love style?
3. Have you developed the habit of happiness?
4. Can you say what you mean and understand what you hear?
5. Have you bridged the gender gap?
6. Do you know how to fight a good fight?
7. Are you and your partner soul mates?

These questions comprise the chapter titles of the main book in this kit.

Also available are the accompanying men's and women's workbooks containing numerous self-tests and exercises for the couple to do on their own and then discuss with each other and maybe even you as their mentors. In addition, the SYMBIS video has proven to be a very effective and fun way for mentors to cover the material and follow it up with personalized questions. This kit also includes a leader's guide with further suggestions on how to use it as a mentor couple, whether one-on-one with a couple or in a small group or classroom setting.

By the way, we also have a version of SYMBIS especially for couples entering a second marriage. *Saving Your Second Marriage Before It Starts* (or SYMBIS-2 for short) includes all of the original seven questions but adds two more:

8. Are you ready for remarriage?
9. Do you know how to blend a family?

Whether just one or both of the partners is coming into the current marriage from a previous marriage, we recommend this resource. It includes the men's and women's workbooks with specific exercises germane to their situation. The same SYMBIS DVD kit contains an additional session for these couples as well.

For couples entering a second marriage, we highly recommend that the marriage mentors working with them also be in a second marriage. Of course, this is not always possible, but the unique challenges for a second marriage — especially if children are involved — can be addressed far more effectively with a mentor couple who has actually been there.

To learn more about the SYMBIS and SYMBIS-2 kits, visit our website at www.RealRelationships.com.

Love Talk:
A Tool for Mentoring Couples
from Good to Great

For mentoring couples who want to focus on helping other couples improve their communication, we developed *Love Talk*, a strategy for going beneath the surface to the root of what causes even the most well-intentioned couples to have conversational meltdowns. The program begins with a brushup on the basics but quickly moves to a revolutionary way of "speaking each other's language like you never have before." It all has to do with discovering your combination of "talk styles." And your talk style is revealed as you learn to accurately answer these four questions:

- Are you an aggressive or passive problem solver?
- Are you influenced more by feelings or facts?
- Are you resistant to or accepting of change?
- Are you a cautious or spontaneous decision maker?

Once each spouse can accurately answer these questions—and that's precisely what the program helps them do—then they will understand how each of them is hardwired differently for conversation. And this insight does not require either partner to change. That's how God made them. Understanding this brings about more patience, grace, and empathy in their conversations. And it immediately explains how they may have ended up in a conversational dead-end and how they can quickly get out of it.

Love Talk also reveals to couples the fundamental conversational differences between men and women, how men tend to analyze while women tend to sympathize. And it also shows couples when to stop talking. This may sound strange, but it's important for couples to know when to clam up.

The *Love Talk* package includes a book, men's and women's workbooks, and a six-session DVD with leader's guide that is especially helpful to marriage mentors who might want to use this one-on-one with their mentorees or with a small group of couples. Another exciting feature of this program is the online Love Talk Indicator. In just ten minutes, a couple can take this assessment and receive a personalized report on their talk style. Their spouse can do the same thing and then the couple can request a "Couples Report" online that combines their profiles and shows them exactly how their two talk styles interact. This assessment can be particularly helpful to process with marriage mentors.

Your Time-Starved Marriage: A Tool for Mentoring Couples from Good to Great

After resolving communication meltdowns, most couples report that finding time together is their top relational need. And yet, there is precious little written about it. When we decided to explore this subject for our own relationship, we couldn't find a single book on the topic. So we did extensive research and came up with our own. And as you might guess, we kept marriage mentors in mind as we developed the program.

For mentoring couples who want to focus on regaining more time for their marriage, we developed a strategy called *Your Time-Starved Marriage*, all about "making meaningful connections while traveling at the speed of life." *Your Time-Starved Marriage* is for couples who are feeling overscheduled and underconnected.

This is not a resource about going back in time to an idealized, preindustrial era where a slower pace romantically resolved all ills for couples. Rather this is a book about real life in the real world. And it's not about being more productive — it's about being more connected.

In addition to showing couples how to battle the busyness monster, we show couples how to discover their unique "time styles." Just as every person is hardwired with a unique talk style, which we explore in *Love Talk* (see the previous appendix) so are we hardwired to experience and use time in a unique and personal way. Though most couples never consider this, once they do, they soon see how it can save them untold hours. Here are a few of the topics covered in *Your Time-Starved Marriage*:

- Time styles: uncovering your unique approach to time
- Priorities: from finding to making time together
- Primetime: maximizing the minutes that matter most
- Time bandits: catching your time-stealers red-handed
- Meals: what's the rush?
- Finances: time is money
- Rest: recouping what you crave

Your Time-Starved Marriage comes with men's and women's workbooks

that contain numerous exercises, ideal for exploring with a marriage mentor couple, as well as a six-session DVD and leader's guide (all forthcoming). And as with *Love Talk*, there is also an online assessment that you can use with couples to accurately assess and explore their unique combination of "time styles."

Couples who want to move from good to great may have plenty of other topics to explore with their mentors, but "time and talk" are a pretty good place to start for launching a mentoring ministry whose focus is on maximizing marriages. To learn more about the *Love Talk* and *Your Time-Starved Marriage* kits, visit our website at www.RealRelationships.com.

I Love You More:
A Tool for Mentoring Couples in Distress

Every marriage, no matter how good, eventually bumps into bad things. Even the best marriages have problems. The *I Love You More* program is designed to show couples how minor and major problems can actually increase a couple's love for one another. Understood properly, problems can become the tipping point for a deeper love between a husband and a wife. In fact, everyday problems can compel a couple to say "I love you more." In other words, the same forces that can chip away at a marriage can become the catalyst for new relational depth and richness — provided a couple makes wise choices.

That's where marriage mentors come in. Hearing from another couple who has experienced a similar problem can become like wings to a couple who is floundering. To see another couple who survived and is now thriving is more than hopeful, it's an inspiration.

The *I Love You More* program includes the main book with the following chapters:

- Introduction: More Today than Yesterday
- Love Is Not Enough
- Why Every Marriage Has Everyday Problems
- Tackle This Problem First ... and All Others Get Easier
- Who Said Sex Was a Problem?
- The Six Subtle Saboteurs of Every Marriage
- How to Solve Any Problem in Five (Not So Easy) Steps
- Joining Your Spirits Like Never Before
- The Good That Comes from a Problem-Solving Marriage

An appendix also contains practical help for a marriage in crisis.

A men's workbook and a women's workbook is available for this program and they are ideally used with the *I Love You More* DVD kit which contains six sessions to be used one-on-one with a mentoree couple or in a small group. You can learn more at www.RealRelationships.com.

How Does Evangelism Factor into Marriage Mentoring?

One of the questions we often receive from an audience of potential marriage mentors relates to evangelism. For years we have said that an effective marriage ministry in the local church is one of the greatest portals for evangelism we have today. And of all the marriage mentors who we know personally, Jim Mueller, at Willow Creek Church in Illinois, and president of Growthtrac.com, is one of the most adept at identifying a couple's spiritual condition and mentoring them toward a saving relationship with Jesus Christ. Jim has a heart for premarriage mentoring and he can point to dozens of couples whom he and his wife, Sheri, have brought to Christ through marriage mentoring.

In fact, we asked Jim to succinctly pinpoint the key elements of this important aspect of marriage mentoring and one of the things he said was, "In real world evangelism, often months must pass before you can have a direct spiritual conversation. Not so in marriage mentoring." Jim has discovered the secrets to meaningful evangelism through marriage mentoring.

"Every couple we've mentored has been ready and open to discuss tough spiritual questions by the second session," says Jim. "God somehow prepares couples relationally—and spiritually—to build this relationship fast. We're still amazed at couples' accelerated willingness to do spiritual business with high vulnerability. The timing is God-orchestrated."

Maybe you're thinking, *I'm not an evangelist.* That's not a problem, according to Jim. What does he recommend? We'll let him tell you in his own words:

DON'T PREQUALIFY

When couples inquire at your church for a ceremony date for their wedding, are you screening out spiritual seekers? Review your process. Church attendance, membership, divorce history, and spiritual condition may not be reasons to say "no" to premarriage mentoring. And building your church attendance or membership may not be a reason to say "yes."

BUILD SPIRITUALITY INTO THE PROCESS

Building the spiritual piece into the premarriage process can be a challenge. It affects everything including wedding inquiries, marriage preparation programs, church policy, and mentoring methodology. Even if you are the "mentoring team," it will take time and effort to get this right. But it's not that hard.

Often it's a strategy shift from assigning and planning a wedding date to a longer term "preparing for a marriage" approach. You'll discover that couples are interested in marriage success—and their spirituality. We just need to be sensitive and intentional, delivering the correct message.

Believe me, before long you'll see a "pattern" of successes. You will become a safety net, often initiating a couple's first spiritual conversation where you mentor and love them toward a decision for Jesus. Imagine marrying these new believers in your church! There's nothing like it.

REMEMBER: RELATIONSHIP IS FIRST

As Mark Mittelberg said in his book *Becoming a Contagious Christian*, "You need to barbecue first!" Don't start your sessions with an agenda. Be open to where the Spirit is steering you, meet the couple where they are, and build trust first. Mentoring is not counseling. It's about guiding and doing life with your couple.

DEFINE BIBLICAL MARRIAGE STANDARDS

What are your standards on remarriage? What if a couple is sexually active or living together? Will you marry non-Christians or unequally yoked couples? Does your church have a married elder's statement? Are staff, elders, and volunteers fully behind these standards? Revisit these areas to know where you stand. [And for our purposes here, we've included two sample marriage preparation policies for your review in appendix 17.]

With a purposeful mentoring program, passion, and prayer you can do this. It will change your couples—and your church.

Spotting Red Flags:
When to Refer the Mentoree Couple

Rob and Karen, married twelve years, volunteered to mentor engaged and newlywed couples in their church. Their first mentoree couple was four months away from their wedding day and this couple was very eager to get married — at least most of the time.

Rob and Karen noticed something strange as they got to know this couple. The young man's mood seemed to vacillate dramatically. Sometimes he was energetic and very positive; other times he was lethargic and depressed.

On one occasion, the young woman came to their mentoring meeting alone, explaining that her fiancé wasn't feeling well. When Rob and Karen inquired further, her eyes began to well up with tears.

"He's the greatest man I've ever met but sometimes he seems so sad that I feel like I'm a terrible person. I mean, if I was a better girlfriend, he wouldn't feel this way, right?"

Whoa! Rob and Karen's caution flag was now a red alert. They knew that something was not right for this engaged couple. As they probed and learned more of the situation, they knew it was beyond their mentoring capabilities. Taking plenty of time to comfort the young woman, they then talked with her about her fiancé's need for professional help. They emphasized that they were not abandoning her and would walk through this process with them.

Being part of a large church, Rob and Karen connected with their counseling center and helped the young man get an appointment with a professional counselor, who diagnosed him as at the beginning stages of "bipolar disorder," or manic depression. As the young man went through treatment, the couple decided to postpone their marriage so he could focus on finding stability in his life.

Think of the heartache Rob and Karen helped this young couple avoid — all because they knew how to spot a red flag and then follow through on getting them the help they needed.

Every effective marriage mentor knows that he or she is not equipped to handle every situation. You may be expertly trained, have a wealth of experience, keep current with research, and routinely pray for wisdom. But there are occasions when a mentoree couple needs assistance that a mentor simply cannot give. We're talking about those issues that subtly or not so subtly move from "normal" to "abnormal."

When to Take Action

Let's face it, you are on the front lines. As marriage mentors, you are likely to be among the first people to know when and if a couple needs serious help that goes beyond marriage mentoring (in the case of major depression, for example). In spite of the continuing stigma of psychological treatment and the belief that families — especially in evangelical circles — should be able to solve their personal problems without outside help, mental health professionals can be of great value in helping hurting couples find the healing comfort of the Holy Spirit.

Below is a list of questions to help you determine whether your mentoree is dealing with an issue that needs professional intervention. If you answer yes to any of these "red flag" issues, it's time to refer:

- Is one of your mentorees painfully silent for long periods and withdrawn socially (even with his or her spouse)?
- Is one of your mentorees quitting a job for no rational reason or making other sudden unexplainable decisions?
- Is one of your mentorees obsessed with exercise and diet to the point that you think she (rarely does this occur in males) might have an eating disorder?
- Is one of your mentorees practicing any form of self-mutilation in the form of cuts or burns?
- Is one of your mentorees showing an excessive fear of a particular family member, other relative, or family friend?
- Does one of your mentorees have long periods of feeling worthless, helpless, guilty, or lethargic? Does he or she suffer from depression?
- Does one of your mentorees blow up with anger? Is he or she a threat to someone's physical well-being, especially the fiancée or spouse and children?

- Does one of your mentorees report hearing voices that others do not hear? Does he or she hallucinate or is he or she out of touch with reality?
- Is one of your mentorees having serious problems with sleep, such as insomnia, repeated wakefulness at night, frequent nightmares, or sleeping too much?
- Does one of your mentorees have morbid thoughts, talk about death a lot? Is he or she suicidal?
- Does one of your mentorees drive while drinking? Do you suspect a problem with excessive drinking or drug use?
- Does one of your mentorees experience relatively brief periods of intense anxiety? Does he or she suffer from panic attacks?

Of course, this is not an exhaustive list of every possible issue that may require professional help but it covers the most common ones.

GETTING YOUR COUPLES THE HELP THEY NEED

If you are working with a couple trying to cope with any of these issues, or any potential form of mental illness, it is incumbent upon you to help them find the professional help their issue deserves.

The following information is designed to help you become an informed consumer and advocate of psychological services for your mentorees. With this in mind, the first item of importance in selecting a psychotherapist is to know the different kinds of qualified professionals. An old joke among practitioners asks, "What's the difference between a psychologist and a psychiatrist?" The answer: "About ten dollars an hour." Of course, differences go far beyond their fees.

Unfortunately, in the United States specifically, almost anyone can put out a shingle and label themselves as a therapist. This term, however, indicates nothing about the person's education and experience. People seeking therapy should never be shy about asking helping professionals about their credentials. It is important to understand the legal and functional distinctions that make each approach unique. You can see the classification of mental health practitioners in the box on page 202.

Types of Mental Health Practitioners

Psychiatrists are medical doctors who have advanced training in mental health and psychopathology. Some specialize in prescribing psychotropic medication and have had little training in psychotherapy or counseling, while others do psychotherapy or psychoanalysis in addition. Certification in psychiatry by the American Board of Psychiatry and Neurology is preferred but not required.

Psychologists hold a PhD, EdD, or a PsyD from an approved institution of higher education. Not all psychologists are trained as counselors or psychotherapists, however.

Clinical psychologists are trained in helping people solve major psychological problems. Licensed by the states in which they practice, clinical psychologists work in a number of settings including hospitals, prisons, clinics, and private practices.

Counseling psychologists usually help people solve psychological problems related to such areas as personal adjustment, marriage, family, career, and school. They are licensed in the same way as clinical psychologists but often work in school settings and in private practices.

Marriage and family therapists become licensed as Marriage, Family, and Child Counselors (MFCC) in most states. Their training and practice is based on a theory of systems rather than a model of individual therapy.

Pastoral counselors are ministers who have been trained primarily in theology but have also acquired education and experience in counseling. They maintain a vision of spiritual wholeness rooted in their belief in the healing power of God. Many have been trained in one of over 350 clinical pastoral education centers in the United States.

Substance abuse counselors help individuals suffering from addictions to drugs and alcohol. They usually work in treatment centers for substance abuse.

In choosing a therapist, your mentoree will want to have a knowledgeable source of information. One of the best sources is people in the helping professions. Physicians, ministers, nurses, and teachers can often provide excellent referrals. Other informational sources include hospitals, community service societies, referral services, and local professional societies. Their information, however, is usually less candid and thus less helpful. Little can be told about the skills and training from a therapist's phone listing, but the yellow pages of the telephone directory do provide another source of information. If your mentoree expresses a concern that the therapist be sympathetic to Christian values and beliefs, a couple of good referral sources can help you:

American Association of Christian Counselors: www.aacc.net

Focus on the Family: www.family.org

Once you have two or three good referrals, the next step for your mentoree is to find out which therapist in your area is the best match for them. As they gather information, here are some questions they may want to ask of the counselor or therapist:

- Are they licensed?
- Do they work with the specific issue of concern on a regular basis?
- What are their credentials?
- At what university did they earn their credentials?
- What professional associations are they accountable to?
- How will they approach the particular problem?
- How long do they expect treatment to take?

In the end it comes down to following one's instincts. And by the way, ultimately this is your mentorees' responsibility, not yours. But you can guide them more effectively with this knowledge.

As we close, we want to underscore once more the fact that, though rare, if you ever suspect one of your mentorees needs help beyond your capabilities, you need to make them aware of that and then do your best to connect them to an appropriate professional. It just might be the most caring thing you ever do as a marriage mentor.

APPENDIXES *for* PASTORS *and* MARRIAGE MENTOR LEADERS

What Every Pastor Needs to Know about Starting a Marriage Mentoring Ministry

Starting with the basic elements of marriage mentoring will benefit every pastor who wants to begin this ministry in the local church. This appendix, in fact, is devoted to doing just that. Here we provide you with the three crucial steps for finding success in a marriage mentoring ministry: recruiting mentors, screening couples, and training couples.

RECRUITING MARRIAGE MENTOR COUPLES

When asked if people wanted to mentor another couple, surveys reveal that 59 percent agree or strongly agree that they'd like to do so. Yet only 25 percent of these couples say they are currently mentoring another couple.[1] In other words, more seasoned couples in the local church *want* to be plugged in and used as mentoring couples but aren't.

So the good news is that motivation isn't a serious problem for most churches that want to start a mentoring ministry. Chances are that you have couples in your care who would like very much to do this. And because you are reading this book, you obviously are motivated as well. The issue is developing a successful program that draws couples into it.

How can you do this? It begins with establishing your mentoring ministry — that is, setting up a structure for mentoring that can be easily described. We help you do this in more detail in part 2 where we describe the marriage mentoring triad of preparing, maximizing, and repairing. The three sides of the triangle encompass the main components of the marriage mentoring ministry and also describe the target group easily.

Recruiting marriage mentors also requires a comfort level with describing it. The following phrase, for example, can quickly convey what marriage mentoring is all about: "Linking seasoned couples with less experienced couples." By using this simple phrase, almost like a mantra when talking with prospective mentors, you will quickly convey the essence of mentoring so that couples "get it."

Additionally, we have produced a forthcoming high-quality DVD tool for recruiting marriage mentors. You'll find a brief promotional piece suitable for showing to the entire congregation as a way of announcing your new ministry. And a longer piece is available to show in classes and even one-on-one with potential marriage mentor couples. With input from dozens of ministers and marriage mentor couples around the country, we've designed a recruitment piece that strategically captures the attention of potential marriage mentors. Here you will see salient sound bites from real-life mentors as well as mentorees. On this same DVD you also will find the information we describe below on training marriage mentors. You can learn more about this tool at www.RealRelationships.com.

SCREENING MARRIAGE MENTOR COUPLES

We'll say it again: not everyone who volunteers to be a mentoring couple should automatically be permitted to do mentoring. We addressed this issue in chapter 2, where we outlined the foundational character qualities that mentoring requires: warmth, genuineness, and empathy. Typically, these are qualities either you possess or you don't. And though they can be cultivated, they are more accurately thought of as natural "leanings" that should be relatively innate for mentors who serve in your program. (Of course, when it comes to "training" mentors, we will have much more to say about honing these attributes.) Chapter 2 also included a bulleted list of caution flags for marriage mentors. You may want to review these once more as one device for screening marriage mentors.

More specific, in-depth instruments you may want to use as screening devices are available in the marriage mentoring section of our website at www.RealRelationships.com.

In addition to these standardized assessments, we know that many churches launching a marriage mentoring program find it helpful to have a relatively simple profile completed by the mentors themselves as a way of quickly gathering essential information. You'll find a sample of this kind of profile in appendix 13 as well as online at www.RealRelationships.com where you can download it. Some churches also find it beneficial to ask potential mentors questions about background, interests, and hobbies (and do the same with mentorees) as a way of matching couples with similar attractions.

By the way, in our experience, the vast majority of couples who volunteer to mentor *are* in a very good place to do so. It is only a small percentage of couples who aren't quite ready to jump into this experience. And if you do face the situation of telling a potential mentoring couple that they don't fit the bill, it's easier than you think.

In fact, a good assessment, like those we point you to on our website, often will do the talking for you. A couple who is not in a healthy place usually will pick up on this from the assessment. Of course, if they need a little nudge you can gently point this out by saying something like, "I'm guessing you two already realize that it might be best to postpone your mentoring activities for a little while." More often than not, this will come as a relief to the couple who is not quite ready for mentoring together.

TRAINING MARRIAGE MENTOR COUPLES

Once you have recruited a marriage mentor couple and "screened" them to be sure they are suitable for mentoring, it's time to train them. We have done quite a bit of work in this area and have, in fact, conducted research studies on training marriage mentors to know for sure what is most helpful.[2]

You've seen in part 3 the eleven skills, or proficiencies, we explore with marriage mentors-in-training. Not only are these skills covered in-depth in this book, but we have also produced a forthcoming training DVD course (with participant workbooks) for mentors to take either in a classroom setting, at a retreat or seminar, or at their own pace at home. Once completed, the mentors can take an online questionnaire and if they can answer a significant portion of the questions correctly they can receive a personalized "certificate of completion." Again, you can learn more about this at www.RealRelationships.com.

CORE DISCUSSION TOPICS

So you've recruited and trained your marriage mentors. Now the question is, what subjects are they going to discuss with their mentorees? As we've said before, every couple is unique and will have their own set of issues that they'd like to explore. But a core group of topics — among them money, communication, sex, and conflict resolution — tend to crop up repeatedly in any marriage relationship. We deal with these in depth in part 2 and, for your convenience, we have summarized them in appendix 1.

NOTES ON SETTING UP A MARRIAGE MENTORING MINISTRY BASED ON THE PREPARING/MAXIMIZING/REPAIRING TRIANGLE

Newlywed and Engaged Couples

Chapter 5 is a great place to start if you're thinking about setting up a marriage mentoring program that focuses specifically on newlywed or engaged couples. You will also want to check out appendix 3, where we describe other resources for this "stage" of marriage, and appendix 17, where we provide two sample church premarital policies for churches which may be considering whether or not to implement such a policy.

A marriage preparation policy will establish a uniform means for making expectations clear for any couple wanting to get married in your church. This may include your policy on how many premarital counseling sessions or classes a couple must attend, or if they are required to meet a certain number of times with a marriage mentor. It also may spell out a specific waiting period of, say, four months from the initial appointment until the wedding date; that the couple needs to commit to a postmarital session with a pastor or mentor; or to abstain from sex and not cohabit until marriage, and so on.

Taking Couples from Good to Great

Again, we've looked at this topic in depth in chapter 6, and explore more resources in appendixes 4 and 5, so we won't add much here. But we want to stress again that a mentoring ministry for maximizing marriages will thrive when there is ample programming—whether it be through seminars, retreats, classes, small group studies, or one on one—that attracts couples to work on their marriages.

To be honest, this side of the marriage mentoring triad is the most neglected in the church. And maybe for good reason. After all, the reparative side's need is glaring and the preparation side is one that is typically the least threatening and most traditionally understood in the church. But don't neglect this important aspect of marriage mentoring. Enrichment is a huge need! This aspect of mentoring is what will keep your congregation healthy, vibrant, and strong. This is what will help your laypeople lead.

Couples in Distress

Setting up a mentoring ministry for couples in distress is one of the most redemptive activities the church can undertake. To instill hope in a marriage that is flagging brings hope to everyone who knows that couple. Such a ministry can come alongside a church's regular counseling ministry and may very well be the best solution for those couples who do not require professional or pastoral counseling. See the resources on this topic in chapter 7, which mentions the fine work of Retrouvaille, and appendix 6 for a program that deals with just this topic.

KEEPING A GOOD THING GOING

Allow us to say a word about the structure and the role of a church staff when it comes to launching and maintaining a successful marriage mentoring ministry. Why? Because sometimes we hear from a church that gets excited about marriage mentoring, launches the program, and then a few months down the line begins to wonder why the initial excitement has dissipated.

The answer, in a single word, is nurture.

The couples who volunteer their time — and their marriage — to be used in this kind of ministry need to be routinely fed. They need to be recognized. Stroked. Appreciated. This doesn't require anything fancy, but it *does* mean you can't forget them.

To ensure that these mentor couples get the nurture they need, we recommend that a minister on staff (or the senior minister in a small church) make this ministry an official part of his or her responsibilities. We can almost hear some of you groan who are reading this. We know you don't need yet another program to oversee. So take a deep breath. This one is low-maintenance and enriching. We suggest you recruit a marriage mentor "champion" or "lead" couple who can serve as your point couple for all-things-marriage-mentoring in your church. Even as you are reading this, that specific couple is probably coming to mind. You know the one. They are sharp. Wise. Healthy. Seasoned. Motivated to help. This couple is the point of the marriage mentoring spear.

As team players, they will guide you as much as you will guide them in caring for and encouraging the mentors in your ministry. They can match mentors with mentorees. Under your supervision, they can facilitate recruitment, screening, and training as well as assist you in the mentors' ongoing nurture. They may, for example, host a quarterly gathering of mentors in your church or help to coordinate an annual retreat for them. In fact, if they so choose, they can even sign up for regular online "marriage mentor champions" helps at our website. We want to augment your care of these special people and their care of the mentors they are coordinating.

TAKING THE FIRST STEP

Some time ago at our own church one of the ministers showed us a cartoon he'd clipped from a magazine for ministers. It was a pastor standing in front of a small group of men and saying: "So far the only thing we have in common is an aversion to singing, socializing, and sharing." The caption above the cartoon read: "The Challenge of Starting a Men's Ministry."

We hope that whatever challenge you might encounter in starting a marriage ministry won't seem as daunting as that! Sure, you may have challenges. Any new program takes a while to gather momentum. But we've interviewed enough pastors and point couples who have launched such programs to tell you—as would they—that it is well worth it. Don't let timidity or fear keep you from taking the first step. Go for it!

Volunteers
and the Local Church

The most comprehensive study on volunteers in the church that we know of asked two fundamental questions.[1] First, why do people volunteer? And second, are they glad they do volunteer? Here's what the study of more than a thousand churchgoing individuals across several denominations said.

The number-one reason people give for volunteering in the local church goes something like this: "I want to put my faith to work in a meaningful way." Or they say it this way: "I want to express my gratitude to God through service in the church." A close-second reason involves the volunteers' love for their local church. "I am a volunteer because there are significant needs to be met, and the church needs help in meeting them."

Sure, there are plenty of other reasons people give for volunteering, but these two top the list and might be summarized as: (1) putting their faith into action, and (2) meeting the church's needs.

Are these volunteers glad they volunteer? You bet. They express feelings of personal growth and tell stories of how they have become better people for having gotten involved as a volunteer. Over all, they are more upbeat and happier about their lives.

Pastor Eric Swanson, in a separate study, surveyed his own church to see if people saw a relationship between ministering to others and spiritual growth.[2] When asked, "To what extent has your ministry or service to others affected your spiritual growth?" 92 percent answered positively. None responded that ministry had a negative effect on their spiritual growth. Sixty-three percent indicated that service was equally significant in their spiritual growth compared to other spiritual disciplines, such as Bible study and prayer. Twenty-four percent responded that ministry or service to others had been "a more significant factor" to their spiritual growth than Bible study or prayer. Over half (58 percent) of those who were not actively ministering to others felt either "not satisfied" or "somewhat satisfied" with their level of spiritual growth.

213

For this reason alone, we felt compelled to include this appendix on volunteering in the local church. After all, marriage mentoring is an act of volunteering and the side effects of this action are too good to ignore. Those who make excuses for not volunteering in this cause are missing out on a great opportunity to put their faith into action, to meet the needs of the local church, and to improve their spiritual growth. Oh, and to lead happier, more meaningful lives.

We admit that people can always find an excuse for not participating at church. In fact, if you poll pastors on their biggest challenges, most will mention their struggle to recruit volunteers—be it for Sunday school classes, ushering, singing in the choir, or, yes, marriage mentoring. So let's take a quick look at some of the most common excuses potential volunteers use and touch on how they relate to marriage mentoring. And more importantly, how they don't really hold water.

I DON'T HAVE THE TIME

This is a big one. And one that may have some merit. After all, who among us has a lot of free time to spare? But then again, when we say we value "giving back," when we know it gives life meaning, why is it that we still don't make the time to do what we often feel called to?

A research project by Darley and Batson at Princeton Theological Seminary in 1973 sheds some light. A group of theology students were told to go across campus to deliver a sermon about the Good Samaritan. As part of the research, some of these students were told that they were late and needed to hurry up. Along their route across campus, Darley and Batson had hired an actor to play the role of a victim who was coughing and obviously suffering.

Ninety percent of the "late" students ignored the needs of the suffering person in their haste to get across campus. As the study reports, "Indeed, on several occasions, a seminary student going to give his talk on the parable of the Good Samaritan literally stepped over the victim as he hurried away!"

Remarkable, isn't it? Yet, believing we are short on time, we might do the very same thing. When you prioritize time over people, this excuse for volunteering almost always wins out.

I'm Not Really Needed

Jackie Mickels of Madrid, Nebraska, tells the story of an "innocent bystander" at a wedding. "After forty-six years of marriage, my husband and I still chuckle about our four-year-old ringbearer's next-day panic when he asked his mother if he had gotten married the day before. 'No,' she reassured him."

His reply: "Then what in the world was I doing up there?"

Ever felt like this ring bearer? Ever felt like you're not really needed? It's a common excuse among potential volunteers. It's not that they even think someone else will do it. They simply seem blind to the need. They don't recognize how their help could remedy a situation because they don't see the need to help.

It's tough to imagine that this excuse could be used when it comes to marriage mentoring, however. After all, if we are ever going to win the war on the skyrocketing divorce rate in the church, not to mention outside the church, we will need to enlist every capable couple we can. The cause is too great to say, "I'm not really needed." The need is too big to sit on the sidelines. When it comes to marriage mentoring, this excuse doesn't stand up. Not by a long shot.

I Don't Have What It Takes

This is probably the most common excuse we hear among potential marriage mentors: "We don't have a perfect marriage." As if that's the prerequisite for being a mentor couple. Of course, we aren't looking for perfect couples. In fact, any couple who thinks they are perfect is, by default, not ready to be a mentoring couple. Why? Because we all have foibles. And paradoxically, it's our weaknesses, our imperfections that enable us to be used by God when he calls us to volunteer.

In the blockbuster book *The Purpose-Driven Life*, Rick Warren has this to say about the excuse of not having what it takes to answer the call of God:

> Abraham was old, Jacob was insecure, Leah was unattractive, Joseph was abused, Moses stuttered, Gideon was poor, Samson was codependent, Rahab was immoral, David had an affair and all kinds of family problems, Elijah was suicidal, Jeremiah was depressed, Jonah was reluctant,

Naomi was a widow, John the Baptist was eccentric to say the least, Peter was impulsive and hot-tempered, Martha worried a lot, the Samaritan woman had several failed marriages, Zacchaeus was unpopular, Thomas had doubts, Paul had poor health, and Timothy was timid. That is quite a variety of misfits, but God used each of them in his service. He will use you too if you stop making excuses.[3]

We couldn't agree more. God will use the couple who doesn't have a perfect marriage to minister to others for that very reason. Sure, there are those couples whose condition will preclude them from mentoring others. But the vast majority of couples in the church today have much to offer other couples—even if they erroneously believe that they don't. Bottom line, this excuse holds very little water.

SOMEONE ELSE WILL DO IT

During the 1960s, when there was no shortage of drama in the nation's courtrooms, one murder case stood alone in its ability to shock the country even though the crime was not as gruesome as some others. The victim was an ordinary girl, neither wealthy nor elite. Her name was Catherine Genovese, the twenty-eight-year-old daughter of Italian-American parents. But to millions of people who read her story when it first appeared in New York City's press, she would forever be remembered as "Kitty" Genovese. What happened to her on that dreadful night in the spring of 1964 would reverberate across the country and generate a national soul-searching that continues all these years later. Her name has become synonymous with what is termed "bystander apathy."

Along a serene, tree-lined street in the Kew Gardens section of Queens, Catherine Genovese began the last walk of her life, returning to her apartment building that night after work. Here's how the *New York Times* reported it the next morning:

> For more than half an hour 38 respectable, law-abiding citizens in Queens watched a killer stalk and stab a woman in three separate attacks.... Twice their chatter and the sudden glow of their bedroom lights interrupted him and frightened him off. Each time he returned, sought her out, and stabbed her again. Not one person telephoned the police during the assault; one witness called after the woman was dead.[4]

Researchers call it the diffusion of responsibility. It's simply a decrease in the amount of personal responsibility one feels when in the presence of many other people. In cases where many people are present during an emergency, it becomes much more likely that any one individual will simply do nothing. Indeed, social psychology research supports the notion that Catherine Genovese had a better chance of survival if she had been attacked in the presence of just one witness.

One can't help but think that the same thing is happening in the deaths of too many marriages. It's understandable that potential volunteers, potential marriage mentors, could fall victim to bystander apathy, thinking someone else will do it. But no one else has. Too many marriages have perished as we've stood helpless. Again, this excuse, while explainable, is no excuse at all.

Nobody Has Ever Asked

Of all the excuses for not volunteering, this one may hold the most merit. In too many churches, too many people go untapped because they simply have not been asked to use their gifts in the right area.

In John Stott's book *One People*, he laments the fact that in many churches laypeople are mainly frozen assets, the unemployed in the labor force. If they could only be assigned the right job, they would undergo a metamorphosis like a worm becoming a butterfly.

It's true. Once a person or couple finds their volunteer fit, they come alive. They literally begin to feel and act differently. Using one's gifts to make a difference does that. It literally infuses one's life with newness. So never let the excuse of never being asked stand in the way of your full potential for a meaningful life. The excuse is too flimsy and your gifts are too desirable.

To sum up, it's clear that the benefits outweigh any cost for a volunteer being involved in a marriage mentoring ministry. And we believe the "boomerang" effect we talked about in chapter 4 will far compensate for the time and energy invested. We see this relationship as a win-win all around, and hope you've caught the vision and passion as you go about (or continue) in your church's marriage mentoring program. Just think of the marriages saved and strengthened!

How to Use the Marriage Mentoring DVD Kit to Train Mentors

We all know that a picture is worth a thousand words. And when it's a "moving picture" the message is even more powerful. That's why we developed a top-notch DVD kit to accompany this book. The DVD features real-life mentors and mentorees, talking about and demonstrating what they do.

To begin with, the DVD includes specific segments that you will find helpful in announcing the launch of your marriage mentoring ministry — a short segment appropriate for showing to the entire congregation as well as to classes or even individuals. It succinctly explains what marriage mentoring is and why it's important. In addition, the DVD provides a salient overview of the marriage mentoring triad, augmented by personal testimonies of its value in the local church. The remaining segments on the DVD provide modules for training marriage mentors. These can be used in a classroom setting, at a retreat or seminar, or even individually at a couple's home. They explain and model — with real-life marriage mentors and mentorees — the essential skills of marriage mentoring.

Along with the DVD resource, we have also developed workbooks for couples to use as they view the DVD programs. This ensures that they internalize the material and learn it at a level that will pay off for them once they begin mentoring. These workbooks are available at bulk discount at www.RealRelationships.com.

The kit also contains a leader's guide that goes into much more detail about how to use the DVD and the accompanying workbooks.

All these products are forthcoming.

Structure for a
Marriage Mentor Ministry

While every church is unique, following is a graphical depiction for structuring your marriage mentoring ministry that may be helpful. As you can see it also incorporates the use of small groups. We've come to believe that a marriage mentor ministry is a tremendous feeder to small groups. And chances are you already have some form of small group program already in place. We offer this diagram (see page 220) as a tool to help you conceptualize how these two ministries can benefit each other. Of course, you can adapt this structure to make it your own and fit the personality and style of your own congregation. And as you do so, we invite you to share what is working for you at www.RealRelationships.com so that other churches can learn from your experience and you can learn from theirs.

Structuring a Marriage Mentoring Ministry

How to Implement the Marriage Mentoring Triad

Pastor

Pastor Recruitment
1. Present the marriage mentoring team model
2. Pastor to recruit marriage mentor lead couple
3. Marriage mentor lead couple to recruit
   three marriage mentor track leaders

Marriage Mentor Lead Couple

Marriage Mentor Lead Couple Responsibilities
1. Spiritual leadership of the marriage triad
2. Recruitment, training, and equipping of marriage mentors
3. Point of contact for funneling couples into triad categories
4. Hosting small group leader training
5. Coordinating marriage enrichment events (retreats, etc.)
6. Certified trainer of assessment tools

Marriage Mentor Track Leaders

"Preparing   "Maximizing   "Repairing
 Track"   Track"   Track"

Marriage Mentor Track Leaders Responsibilities
1. Provide supervision of their respective triad track
2. Become certified in their triad track
3. Point of contact for couples seeking track training
4. Recruit small group leaders for track
5. Certified trainer of track assessment tools
6. Promote track throughout the church

Small Group Couple Responsibilities
1. Take part in small group leadership track training
2. Take the respective track assessment and expanded diagnostic
3. Recruit small group participants for their small group
4. Promote track throughout the church
5. Commit to replicate their group every 18 months
   (raising up a small group leader couple from their group)

Small Group Leaders

"Preparing Track"   "Maximizing Track"   "Repairing Track"
Small Group Leaders   Small Group Leaders   Small Group Leaders

Marriage Mentor Application Form

This form is to be completed by each person in a couple.

Name: _____

Address: _____

City: _____ State: _____ Zip Code: _____

Home Phone: _____ Cell Phone: _____

Email: _____

Wedding anniversary (including year): _____

Children? Y N   If yes, provide ages and gender: _____

Previously married? Y N   If yes, please explain: _____

How motivated are you to become a marriage mentor?   1   2   3   4   5   6   7   8   9   10
                                                       Very Little   Very Much

Why do you want to be a marriage mentor? _____
_____

Under which of these categories are you most interested in being a marriage mentor?
                                        Very Little   Very Much

Preparing for Marriage   1   2   3   4   5   6   7

Maximizing Marriages   1   2   3   4   5   6   7

Repairing Marriages   1   2   3   4   5   6   7

What concerns or fears do you have about becoming a marriage mentor? _____
_____

Are you willing to participate in a bit of training to become a marriage mentor?   Y   N

How would you rate your marriage?   1   2   3   4   5   6   7   8   9   10
                                             Not Happy   Very Happy

What will make you a particularly good marriage mentor (note any skills, education, life experience, challenges you've overcome, etc.)?
_____

Please describe the most outstanding crisis you have experienced as a couple and how you dealt with it.
_____
_____

How would you rate your individual spiritual life   1   2   3   4   5   6   7   8   9   10
(i.e., your relationship with God)?   Nonexistent   Strong

Please provide your Christian testimony: _____
_____
_____

If you are not selected to be a marriage mentor at this time, are you willing to be considered again later?   Y   N

PLEASE NOTE: Full-size form is available for download as a PDF at www.RealRelationships.com.

221

Marriage Mentoree Application Form

We're so glad you are interested in being matched with a marriage mentor couple who will commit to walking alongside you in your marriage. You're making a great decision to get involved in this program. Please take a moment to complete this brief form so we can make the best match possible for you.

Name: _____

Address: _____

City: _____ State: _____ Zip Code: _____

Home Phone: _____ Cell Phone: _____

Email: _____

Wedding anniversary (including year) or projected wedding date: _____

Children? Y N   If yes, provide ages and gender: _____

Previously married? Y N   If yes, please explain: _____

How would you rate your marriage?

1   2   3   4   5   6   7   8   9   10
Not Happy   Very Happy

For which category are you seeking a marriage mentor?

☐ Preparing for marriage
☐ Maximizing your marriage
☐ Repairing your marriage

In specific terms, what are you hoping that a marriage mentor couple will do for you? _____

_____

Do you have any unusual scheduling issues that may impact when you can meet with your mentors?

_____

Thank you for providing us with this information.

Marriage Mentor Meeting Report Form for the Mentoree Couple

Thanks for taking a moment to fill out this form. Occasionally it is helpful to our mentoring ministry to know how your mentor meetings are going and this form is a means of gathering this information.

Date: _____

Your Names: _____

Names of Your Mentor Couple: _____

What is the primary focus on your mentoring experience (e.g., preparing, maximizing, repairing)? _____
_____

How many times have you met with your mentor couple? _____

Where do you usually meet? _____

In general, how helpful is this mentoring relationship to you?   1   2   3   4   5   6   7   8   9   10
                                                              Not Helpful   Very Helpful

How confident are you in your mentors' ability to help you?   1   2   3   4   5   6   7   8   9   10
                                                           Not Confident   Very Confident

What would you like us to know about your mentoring experience? _____
_____

Would you like someone in our ministry to contact you for any reason? If so, please explain and provide your contact information.

_____

_____

_____

Thank you for providing us with this information.

PLEASE NOTE: Full-size form is available for download as a PDF at
www.RealRelationships.com.

Marriage Mentor Meeting Report Form for the Mentor Couple

Thanks for taking a moment to fill out this form. It is helpful to our mentoring ministry to know about your experience so that we can serve you in this important effort.

Date: _____

Your Names: _____

Names of Your Mentoree Couple: _____

What is the primary focus on your mentoring experience (e.g., preparing, maximizing, repairing)?_____

_____

How many times have you met with your mentoree couple?_____

Where do you usually meet? _____

In general, how would you describe your mentoring
relationship (i.e., rapport) with this couple?   1   2   3   4   5   6   7   8   9   10
                                                  Not So Good   Very Good

How helpful do you think your mentoring is to this couple??   1   2   3   4   5   6   7   8   9   10
                                                             Not Helpful   Very Helpful

What's the toughest part about mentoring this couple? _____

_____

What could we do to make your mentoring process better? _____

_____

What would you like us to know about your mentoring experience with this couple?_____

_____

Would you like someone in our ministry to contact you for any reason? If so, please explain and provide your
contact information.

_____

_____

Thank you for providing us with this information.

PLEASE NOTE: Full-size form is available for download as a PDF at
www.RealRelationships.com.

224

Two Samples of Marriage Preparation Policies

SAMPLE 1

Marriage and Family Agreement — Principles and Specifics

Representing various Christian faith communities, we share a common concern regarding marriage, family life, and the overall relational health of the community.

We believe:

- God has provided in the Scriptures principles for people to establish, develop, and foster healthy relationships.

- God has established the covenant of marriage between a man and a woman, intended marriage to be a mutually healthy and loving relationship, and provided the scriptural insights for every marriage to flourish.

- God has provided in the Scriptures keys for every parent to establish and raise a healthy family, that in turn gives every child a stable foundation to grow upon, excel from, and in the future, replicate as they marry and begin their own family.

- God has called us as shepherds of Christian congregations and religious leaders to the community to uphold biblical standards for marriages, families, and healthy relationships.

- God has given the community of churches the responsibility to invest in the future generation of marriage; prepare couples for marriage; empower marriages, parents, and families; and reconstruct hurting marriages, families, and individuals to raise the relational and spiritual health of the community.

Therefore, we will:

- Urge young people and single adults to practice sexual purity in their relationships. We will facilitate opportunities to make a public pledge for abstinence, and for previously sexually active people to make a pledge for secondary virginity. We will provide the tools and resources to help them make healthy choices, ensuring success in their present and future relationships, whether it be a lifetime of marriage or singleness.

- Offer seriously dating couples the opportunity to invest themselves in discovering their "marriage readiness" prior to engagement.

- Require engaged couples to attend at least eight hours worth of premarital education (either in class or one-on-one setting) over a minimum of six months. Included in this time will be instruction on marriage, biblical insights to grow their marriage, and a relational inventory to help evaluate the relationship of the couple.
- Advocate to married couples, parents, families, and individuals the importance of increasing in relational health by providing or promoting relationship-empowering retreats, conferences, workshops, and resources, and also highly encouraging mentoring relationships.
- Provide continuing assistance to reconstruct hurting marriages, fragile families, and distressed individuals to complete relational health by promoting counseling, classes, retreats, and other resources that focus on biblical approaches of reconciliation, mediation, restoration, and spiritual wholeness.
- Equip seasoned couples, parents, and individuals to mentor newlyweds, new parents, single parents, fragile families, and others who could gain from their relational insights and experiences.
- Encourage church leaders to broaden their knowledge and expertise in areas of relational health, as well as expand the healthy relationships ministries available to the church community and community at large.
- Encourage one another as clergy to model strong marriages and healthy families to our congregations.
- Cooperate with other congregations and organizations to create a cultural climate to assist marriages and families to develop and grow to their full potential, therefore raising the relational health of the community.

We recognize that this Marriage and Family Agreement establishes minimum, baseline standards, with the intention that each church will implement its own, more specific policies. While unusual circumstances arise on occasion that necessitate variance from the details of this agreement, we are committed to practices that are consistent with and within the spirit of this Marriage and Family Agreement.

Families Northwest created this Marriage & Family Agreement (MFA). Duplication in part or in its entirety is allowed. Please contact Families Northwest (888.923.2645 or familiesnorthwest.org) with any questions.

SAMPLE 2

Marriage and Family Agreement— Scripture References and Principles

We believe:

- God desires for all individuals to be in relationship with him and to have healthy relationships with other individuals, with family members, and with one's spouse. (Gen. 2:18–25)

- God has established marriage for the welfare and happiness of the human family, and the society at large. Married couples experience all that is intended for their relationship when God is at the center of their lives, individually and as a couple. Marriage is the outward and visible sign of a lifelong commitment between a man and a woman. (Gen. 2:18–25; Matt. 19:4–6; Heb. 13:4)

- God's initial plan for children to be raised in a home with a loving and caring mother and father, united in marriage, is the ideal situation for their overall health and well-being. In family situations where one or both parents are absent, God calls himself a "Father to the fatherless," standing in the gap to supply love, hope, and support for children. (Ps. 128:1–6; Ps. 68:5–6)

- God has a high calling for parents to model virtuous behavior, to teach their children in all areas of life, to edify children in the learning and understanding of God and his ways, and to equip children with the principles for healthy relationships. (Deut 6:4–9; Eph 6:1–4; 1 Thess. 4:1–8)

- God has given Christian congregations the responsibility to foster lasting and joyful marital unions, empower strong and healthy families, minister to hurting individuals, provide hope for struggling marriages and fragile families, and provide an environment for deepening healthy relationships. (Heb. 10:24–25; 1 Thess. 4:3–4)

Therefore, we will:

- Uphold the timeless and proven standards for healthy marriages and families, and the principles to raise the overall relational health of our community.

- Invest in the future generation of marriage by supplying young people and single adults with the knowledge and tools to grow healthy relationships with people of the opposite sex, reserve sexual expression for marriage, and provide singles the fundamentals that lead to future relational success.

- Prepare engaged and seriously dating couples for marriage by providing ample opportunities for them to invest themselves in the work of discovering more about one another, assessing the health of their relationship, providing tools to enhance their future marriage relationship, and instructing them in the foundational truths of God's blueprint for marriage.

- Empower couples, parents, families, and individuals by providing retreats, conferences, workshops, and resources to increase relational health. This allows: couples to deepen their marriage relationship, parents to enhance their time and interaction with their children, families to increase the quality of their relationship, and individuals to thrive in becoming spiritually and relationally complete.

- Reconstruct hurting marriages, fragile families, and distressed individuals to complete relational health by focusing on biblical approaches of reconciliation, mediation, and restoration in an atmosphere of grace, forgiveness, accountability, and hope, uplifting the fact that the Lord is "the God of second chances."

- Equip older married couples to mentor younger couples, parents who have effectively lived out any of the various parenting dynamics to mentor those currently going down a similar path, and families to mentor younger, similar families. Church leaders will also be provided with opportunities to broaden their knowledge and expertise in areas of relational health.

- Network together to supply a variety of resources to couples, families, and individuals that will increase the number of marriages that last a lifetime, enhance the life of families, and perpetuate an environment of relational and spiritual health in our community.

Families Northwest created this Marriage & Family Agreement (MFA).
Duplication in part or in its entirety is allowed. Please contact Families Northwest
(888.923.2645 or familiesnorthwest.org) with any questions.

NOTES

INTRODUCTION: THE SLEEPING GIANT IN THE CHURCH

1. Cf. Thom S. Rainer, *Breakout Churches* (Grand Rapids, Mich.: Zondervan, 2005), 13.
2. Shane Fookes, "Marriage and Family Mentoring," *Family Life* white paper (2004), 4.

CHAPTER 1: WHAT MARRIAGE MENTORING IS AND ISN'T

1. Erik Johnson, "How to Be an Effective Mentor," *Leadership Journal* (spring 2000).
2. Leslie Parrott, *Motivating Volunteers in the Local Church* (Kansas City, Mo.: Beacon Hill Press, 1991).

CHAPTER 2: CAN ANYONE BE A MARRIAGE MENTOR?

1. Miriam Arond and Samuel L. Pauker, *The First Year of Marriage* (New York: Warner Books, 1987).

CHAPTER 3: COMMON PITFALLS OF BEGINNING MARRIAGE MENTORS

1. J. S. Ripley, L. Parrott, E. L. Worthington, L. Parrott, and C. Smith, "An Initial Empirical Examination of the Parrotts' Marriage Mentoring: Training the Program Coordinators," *Marriage and Family: A Christian Journal* 4, no. 1, 77–94.
2. Henry Cloud and John Townsend, *Boundaries* (Grand Rapids, Mich.: Zondervan, 1992).
3. C. R. Rogers, *On Becoming a Person* (Boston: Houghton Mifflin, 1961), 90.

CHAPTER 5: PREPARING: MENTORING ENGAGED AND NEWLYWED COUPLES

1. Steven Wages, "A Formative and Summative Evaluation of a Marriage Preparation Program Using Mentor Couples" (PhD diss., Florida State University, 2002).
2. D. H. Olson and A. K. Olson, "PREPARE/ENRICH Program: Version 2000," in *Preventive Approaches in Couples Therapy*, ed. R. Berger and M. T. Hannah (Philadelphia: Brunner/Mazel, 2000), 196–216.
3. M. D. Bramlett and W. D. Mosher, "First Marriage Dissolution, Divorce, and Remarriage," DHHS Publication No. PHS 2001-1250 01-0384 (Hyattsville, Md.: U.S. Department of Health and Human Services, 2001).

CHAPTER 6: MAXIMIZING: MENTORING COUPLES FROM GOOD TO GREAT

1. J. J. Gottman and N. Silver, *The Seven Principles for Making Marriage Work* (New York: Crown, 1999).
2. Greg Clark, "Good Questions, Great Answers," *Fast Company* (October 2001), 90.

CHAPTER 7: REPAIRING: MENTORING COUPLES IN DISTRESS

1. Anyone suffering from addiction has a serious problem that requires professional intervention. If you or your spouse is struggling with alcohol or drug abuse or dependence of any kind, please realize that this is not a problem that will gradually go away on its own. If you have already tried outpatient treatment programs and they have been unsuccessful, intensive treatment by a professionally trained staff in a hospital setting is likely needed. In addition, many recovering addicts find tremendous support in staying with their sobriety through psychoeducational programs, the largest and most widely known of which is Alcoholics Anonymous with more than a million members (see your local telephone directory). Their Twelve Steps and "one-day-at-a-time" philosophy has been successfully applied to numerous addictions.
2. K. S. Peterson, "Affairs," *USA Today*, December 21, 1998.
3. Frank Pittman, *Private Lies: Infidelity and the Betrayal of Intimacy* (New York: Norton, 1989), 121–25.
4. Henry Virkler, *Broken Promises* (Waco, Tex.: Word, 1992), 230.
5. Beth Cooper-Hilbert, "The Infertility Crisis," *Networker*, November/December 1999, 65–76.
6. Eventually, about 50 percent of those couples will conceive and bear a child while the remaining couples grapple with the dilemma of adoption.
7. J. S. Ripley, L. Parrott, E. L. Worthington, L. Parrott, and C. Smith, "An Initial Empirical Examination of the Parrotts' Marriage Mentoring: Training the Program Coordinators," *Marriage and Family: A Christian Journal* 4, no. 1, 77–94.

CHAPTER 8: BUILDING RAPPORT

1. David A. Stoddard, *The Heart of Mentoring* (Colorado Springs: NavPress, 2003), 66.

CHAPTER 9: WALKING IN ANOTHER COUPLE'S SHOES

1. M. Voboril, "A Weighty Issue," *Newsday*, April 16, 2000.
2. T. Connellan, *Inside the Magic Kingdom* (Atlanta: Bard Press, 1997).
3. R. W. Levenson and A. M. Fuef, "Physiological Aspects of Emotional Knowledge and Rapport," in *Empathic Accuracy*, ed. William Ickes (New York: Guilford Press, 1997).
4. D. Goleman, *Working with Emotional Intelligence* (New York: Bantam, 1998), 136.

CHAPTER 11: AGREEING ON OUTCOMES

1. Max De Pree, "Creative Leadership," *Leader to Leader* 20 (spring 2001): 10–13.
2. Charles Paul Conn in "Making It Happen," *Christianity Today* 32, no. 13.

CHAPTER 12: ASKING MEANINGFUL QUESTIONS

1. Conrad Gempf, *Jesus Asked* (Grand Rapids, Mich.: Zondervan, 2003), 19.

CHAPTER 13: LISTENING AGGRESSIVELY

1. Michael Abrashoff, *It's Your Ship* (New York: Warner Business Books, 2002), 33.

CHAPTER 15: TELLING YOUR STORIES

1. K. M. Sheldon, R. M. Ryan, L. J. Rawsthorne, and B. Ilardi, "Trait Self and True Self," *Journal of Personality and Social Psychology* 73, 1380–93.
2. Henri Nouwen, *Leadership Journal* 2, no. 4.

Chapter 17: Staying Sharp and Refreshed

1. Stephen R. Covey, *The Seven Habits of Highly Effective People* (New York: Simon & Schuster, 1989), 287.
2. William P. Farley, "The Indispensable Virtue," *Discipleship Journal* (Issue 125), 24.
3. Diana Burrell, "Working Hard Can Be Hazardous to Your Holidays," *Psychology Today* (July 2001).
4. Robyn D. Clarke, *Black Enterprise*, December 1, 1999.
5. *The News Letter* (Farmington Hills, Mich.), August 31, 2004.
6. Rodney Clapp, *Marriage Partnership* 5, no. 2.
7. Christianity has a long tradition of Sabbath observance, so a revitalized Sabbath is more a reclaiming of the Christian birthright than the self-conscious adoption of something Jewish. Jesus observed Shabbat, even as he challenged the specifics of Mosaic Sabbath law, and since at least the year 321, when Constantine declared Sunday as Sabbath for all his empire, Christians have understood the Sabbath as a day for rest, communal worship, and celebration.
8. As he writes in his letter to the Colossians (2:16–17), "Therefore do not let anyone judge you ... with regard to a religious festival, a New Moon celebration or a Sabbath day. These are a shadow of the things that were to come; the reality, however, is found in Christ." And Jesus, when rebuked by the Pharisees for plucking grain from a field on Shabbat, criticizes those who would make a fetish of Sabbath observance, insisting that "the Sabbath was made for man, not man for the Sabbath" (Mark 2:27).
9. Judaism speaks of a *neshamah yeteirah*, an extra soul that comes to dwell in you on the Sabbath but departs once the week begins.

Chapter 18: Being Yourself and Going with the Flow

1. Wayne Cordeiro, "A Personal Relationship," *Preaching Today*, audio no. 225.
2. B. Fredrickson, "The Role of Positive Emotions in Positive Psychology," *American Psychologist* 56 (2001): 218–226.
3. Henri Nouwen, *The Wounded Healer* (New York: Doubleday, 1972).

Appendix 9: What Every Pastor Needs to Know about Starting a Marriage Mentoring Ministry

1. Shane Fookes, "Marriage and Family Mentoring," *Family Life* white paper (2004), 5.
2. J. S. Ripley, L. Parrott, E. L. Worthington, L. Parrott, and C. Smith, "An Initial Empirical Examination of the Parrotts' Marriage Mentoring: Training the program Coordinators," *Marriage and Family: A Christian Journal* 4, no. 1, 77–94.

Appendix 10: Volunteers and the Local Church

1. Robert Farrar, "Factors Affecting Volunteerism in Church-Related Activities" (PhD diss., University of Houston, 1985).
2. Eric Swanson, "What You Get from Giving," *Leadership Journal* (spring 2003), 37.
3. Rick Warren, *The Purpose-Driven Life* (Grand Rapids, Mich.: Zondervan, 2002), 233.
4. Martin Gansberg, "Thirty-Eight Who Saw Murder Didn't Call the Police" *New York Times*, March 27, 1964.

INDEX

This Book Is Best Used With:

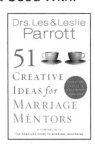

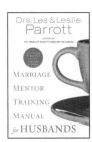

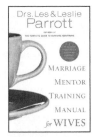

Complete Resource Kit for Marriage Mentoring	51 Creative Ideas for Marriage Mentors	Marriage Mentor Training Manual for Husbands	Marriage Mentor Training Manual for Wives
Curriculum Kit	Softcover	Softcover	Softcover
0-310-27110-X	0-310-27047-2	0-310-27165-7	0-310-27125-8

PREPARE

Saving Your Marriage Before It Starts: Seven Questions to Ask Before (and After) You Marry

Drs. Les and Leslie Parrott

Do you long for real, honest advice from a couple who knows the hopes and struggles of today's couples? Do you want to build a marriage that will last a lifetime? *Saving Your Marriage Before It Starts* shows engaged couples and newlyweds how they can identify and overcome stumbling blocks to a healthy marriage.

Marriage Kit: 0-310-20451-8
Workbook for Men: 0-310-48731-5

Hardcover: 0-310-49240-8
Workbook for Women: 0-310-48741-2

MAXIMIZE

Love Talk: Speak Each Other's Language Like You Never Have Before

Drs. Les and Leslie Parrott

Couples consistently name "improved communication" as the greatest need in their relationships. *Love Talk* is a deep yet simple plan full of new insights that will revolutionize communication in love relationships.

Hardcover: 0-310-24596-6
Workbook for Men: 0-310-26216-7

DVD: 0-310-26467-7
Workbook for Women: 0-310-26213-5

REPAIR

I Love You More: How Everyday Problems Can Strengthen Your Marriage

Drs. Les and Leslie Parrott

I Love You More explores how a marriage survives and thrives when a couple learns to use problems to boost their love life, to literally love each other more.

Softcover: 0-310-25738-7
Workbook for Men: 0-310-26275-5

DVD: 0-310-26582-7
Workbook for Women: 0-310-26276-3

Interested in hosting the Parrotts for one of their highly acclaimed seminars? It's easy. Just visit www.RealRelationships.com to learn more and complete a speaking request form.

Les and Leslie speak to thousands in dozens of cities annually. They are entertaining, thought-provoking, and immeasurably practical. One minute you'll be laughing and the next you'll sit still in silence as they open your eyes to how you can make your relationship all it's meant to be.

"I've personally benefited from the Parrotts' seminar. You can't afford to miss it."

GARY SMALLEY

"Les and Leslie's seminars can make the difference between you having winning relationships and disagreeable ones."

ZIG ZIGLAR

"The Parrotts will revolutionize your relationships."

JOSH MCDOWELL

"Without a doubt, Les and Leslie are the best at what they do and they will help you become a success where it counts most."

JOHN C. MAXWELL

Learn more about the Parrotts' "Becoming
Soul Mates Seminar" and their new "Love Talk Seminar."

*Click on www.RealRelationships.com
to bring them to your community.*